TEACH LIKE A DJ

B. J. Mercer

Copyright © 2018 B. J. Mercer

All rights reserved.

ISBN: 1986482073
ISBN-13: 978-1986482073

DEDICATION

Jim and Wanda Mercer

CONTENTS

1	BJ the DJ	1
2	Know Your Demo	4
3	The Show	15
4	Show Prep	27
5	The Studio	47
6	Sales	61
7	Marketing	71
8	Promotions	82
9	Engineers	92
10	Showtime!	105
	Acknowledgments	130

1 BJ THE DJ

"Here's a story about a guy who played football, lost his marbles, and became a rock and roll DJ."

THAT WAS AN ACTUAL audio clip that played on-air during my first radio hosting gig. Only a few questioned why I would quit football with two years of eligibility remaining to host a radio show.

I was entering my junior year as a free safety at Tarleton State University when I was given the opportunity to host my own afternoon show. The show would air weekdays from three to seven on *The Classic Rock Station*, KCUB 98.3 FM, in Stephenville, Texas. I guess most believed it was the right move for me to make at that time. I was a good football player, but, I already had three years of part-time radio experience, and I knew that a career in radio lay in my future. At twenty-one years old, I was pretty sure I had the greatest job in the world.

Seven years later, I would be asked a more ardent question by everyone who knew my radio background. "Why on earth would you leave a career as a radio DJ to become a teacher?" Students, teachers, colleagues, administrators, friends, family, and the UPS guy all asked with confusion and shocked expressions as if I was searching for ways to punish myself for my good fortune.

The answer to that question was complicated, and exacerbated by the fact that 2008 wasn't the best time to be looking for promotions in any field—especially radio. A better, more quality question to investigate is, "Why have you not returned to radio after teaching for nine years?" That answer is my inspiration and motivation for writing this book, *Teach Like a DJ*.

Doc Brown Moment
My first day of teaching was the day I learned that I'd one day write this book. I realized I'd been preparing to be a teacher for my entire radio career.

Radio requires tremendous focus and energy to distill the most relevant information for your audience and present it in the most engaging way possible. You have to keep them listening, tuned in, and wanting more. All your material, from celebrity news, sports, and give-a-ways, serves to make every second of airtime as full and engaging as possible.

Sales, marketing, promotions, producing, and the daily ritual of providing specific content on-air, for a specific demographic, translated seamlessly to the classroom. The way that producers and

DJs use new audio, video, and web technologies to engage on and off the air, I introduced the same to stimulate multiple types of student learners all at once.

I was wrong about only one thing. All of those incredible years working in radio under the impression that I was following my dream, my passion, and that I had the best job in the world, were false. As a classroom teacher of Communication Applications at a Terrell, Texas high school, I finally realized my calling, my purpose, and my true passion: I am a classroom teacher and now I really do have the greatest job in the world.

This is an epic tale of adventure. A journey filled with ups and downs. You will laugh, you will cry. (Well, I laughed and cried plenty throughout this noble tale.) I want you to see the parallels between what DJs do on a daily basis, and how teachers can use strategies and techniques to approach engaging students in the classroom. Teach like a radio producer and on-air personality to be an even better educator, and make sure our students are engaged at the highest level, tuned in, and wanting more!

Some names have been changed to protect the guilty. The helpful ones along the way will be praised for their excellence. Quiet in the studio; coming at you in 3, 2, 1, go!

2 KNOW YOUR DEMO

"Adapt your instruction for the student, not the student for your instruction."

RADIO STATIONS HAVE a target demographic. All on-air content is created, produced, and broadcast to appeal to the demographic (demo). To teach like a DJ, you need to make sure all of your content is created, produced, and broadcast with the goal of reaching and appealing to your students.

Knowing your demo in the classroom means knowing your students. You need to get to know each and every one of your students individually: their personalities, dreams, goals, talents, aspirations, challenges, and inspirations. Only once you've really heard them, can they hear you.

Caller Number Seven Doesn't Always Win
I arrived at Mix 102.9 with eight years of radio experience. I had

worked in five or so different radio formats surviving as many demographics, so I felt comfortable incorporating my philosophy into broadcasting and producing for yet another demographic. It may sound challenging, but if you start down each new path with your target demographic in mind, you are always headed the right direction.

For the most part, as a first time Morning Show Producer for one of the highest-rated shows (in the fifth-largest market) in the country, I was still doing what I loved and living my dream. Mix 102.9, recently rebranded "Now 102.9" plays a mix of the eighties, nineties, and current adult-contemporary music. The selection is further limited to specific songs, styles, types, genres, and artists. Not only the music, but the on-air personalities, website, commercials, audio production, prizes content, and games are curated for the target demographic. Phone calls are screened to favor women. Only one male winner per every three females win on the air. Same for the number of live callers broadcast during listener interaction, games, and show parts.

The majority of my radio career I was a classic rock DJ. Without a doubt, a classic rock audience requires a completely different prize closet than the one my new, predominantly female demographic would appreciate. We had already identified the demographics of our audience, but that information does little to teach you how to reach the demographic effectively. I had to study and learn this new female demographic. I had to research, learn what appeals to them, and really get to know a truly challenging demographic: women.

In all of my radio experience, I had not produced a show for a women's demographic. I especially had no experience with the women in and around Dallas. If I was really going to reach this demographic and ensure ideas and content were piquing and promoting their interests. I had to know more about this demographic. What I learned changed my strategy significantly.

What Women Want

For the sake of the show, our demographic, and a quality on-air bit, first I tried the Mel Gibson technique. I had full makeup applied by a professional, a dress, and high heels for good measure, and went on a shopping spree at a grocery store to better understand what our demographic goes through daily. Another time, a listener won the chance to pick my Halloween costume. I ended up dressed like a beautiful fairy and tasked with trick-or-treating in the middle of Dallas, days before Halloween.

If the ultimate goal was making sure our female audience knew I was committed to them, then I'm sure it was the right thing to do for the demo. Research showed they also liked handbags and stilettos, so we would find creative ways to give them away. I am talking about the good stuff, not the knock-off stuff. If we were giving away a pair of high heels, there was a good chance they would have red bottoms. (Watch out Christian Louboutin!)

DJs design their shows with the demographic top of mind during every second of airtime. Knowing your demo, and creating content specific to their interests and needs, will lay the foundation for a successful show. Understanding the difference between *identifying* your demographic and *really knowing* your demographic will help you take leaps and bounds toward reaching and engaging your students.

Golden Globe and Academy Award Winner Ryan Bingham

I think it is proper etiquette to introduce Ryan via his well-deserved accolades, but I knew Ryan before he recorded his first song. In fact, I recorded his first song.

Ryan moved to Stephenville, Texas in high school. We were in the same grade. I was already working part-time at a local radio station. Ryan was a bull rider, worked on our friend's ranch, and liked to sing and play guitar. He was a good friend and a hard worker, with a big heart and bigger dreams.

Ryan faced real challenges growing up. He moved often, and there were periods when just he and his sister had to rely on each other. He had it tougher than most, but you would never know it by his personality and smile.

He is a natural with the guitar and has a one-of-a-kind voice. In the spring of 1999, I invited him to stop by the radio station and record a few songs. It just seemed like the right thing to do at the time. I had access to a studio, and he had talent. He was already passionate about playing music. It was in his soul, you could tell. We knew it could help him get more gigs, and I could play producer. Ryan needed a demo tape to share with clubs from

Stephenville to Dallas / Fort Worth in order to book some live shows.

After I finished running the board for the Texas Ranger broadcast one evening, Ryan showed up at the station with guitar in hand. In less than an hour, it was a wrap. A cassette tape, with three songs produced. Ryan had recorded his first demo tape. We were proud. Fortunately, he had plenty of raw talent to cover up any mistakes I may have made producing. We went on to celebrate the new demo release party at his house. He taught me a few songs on the guitar. We even invited some girls over to celebrate with us. The girls never showed up.

Ryan would go on to fail his senior English class that spring. He would not graduate with our class of 1999. Ryan would retake his senior English class the following year and graduate with the class of 2000. Mrs. Muncy, an English teacher at Stephenville High School at the time, made sure he was able to walk across the stage with the next graduating class. Ryan started a college career at Tarleton State University, where he joined the rodeo team as a bull rider and continued to write music.

Despite the senior-year setback, Ryan Bingham was fearless. Eventually, after touring in Europe, and making a move to California, he grew a significant following. In 2008, Ryan was asked to write and perform a song for a new movie. The title track for the movie *Crazy Heart*. The song won a Golden Globe, and the Oscar for Best Original Song.

Ryan Bingham should not have failed high school English.

His instructor did not design instruction with learning experiences that engaged and promote his interests, abilities, and passions. Teachers should be fluid and flexible when engaging their students, and allow the students to discover the essential knowledge and skills in ways that are more creative, innovative, real, and encompassing.

Being flexible enough to adapt to any audience ensures that all content is designed for that audiences' interests, and provides immediate results in the classroom. As a teacher, you should not force your students to fit your mode of instruction, you should adjust your instruction to fit your students.

A New Demo

The new classroom audience would prove to be the most challenging demographic of all, and in a market even smaller than the first radio station I worked at in Stephenville, Texas. A market where we once gave a traffic report about a shoe in the middle of the road, to an audience small enough to recognize the shoe from the report, and who provided listener traffic updates regarding the shoe. More on this story later. Stay tuned.

The new demographic would be a captive audience, meaning they were trapped in room 111 at Terrell High School for 49-minute periods. An audience between fourteen and twenty-four students before the budget cuts of 2010, and twenty-five to thirty-two students after the cuts. The demographic would comprise the greatest mix of my career: teenage boys and girls of multiple ethnicities, backgrounds, and grade levels. I know that big market executives would like to place all teenagers in the same category, but I'm here to tell you that the greatest differences in demographics are found in that small age range.

As a radio DJ, I was often hired to host events, parties, festivals, and dances. A few years in, I realized high school dances were the most challenging events to work. I had endured navigating a bridezilla, or a stressed-out Maid of Honor through an entire year of planning, but, to this day, if you ask me to DJ a high school dance you would need to start saving your money now. Even if you are the most incredible DJ on the planet (and in the history of the world), a high school dance is a tough demo. It does not matter what song, dance, or game you play, someone will hate it. Most likely, an entire group is going to hate it, tell you about it, and provide unsolicited advice on how they would fix the issue. Most of these events have The One Who Knows It All, or The Person Who Used to Be a DJ, and The One Who Insists you Play Metallica as you are looking out over a full dance floor of couples and cowboy hats dancing their best two-step.

You need to eat, sleep, and breathe your demographic. Study them. Know their habits, rituals, strengths, and weaknesses. Know the latest hip-hop dance. Know the top five songs on the Billboard chart. Know the trending YouTube videos, and popular memes. Be careful too. Early in my career, it was appropriate to reference Miley Cyrus during instruction (in her Hannah Montana days). Today, maybe not. You need to stay current.

The dynamic range of ages, experiences, and backgrounds native to high school or middle school demographics create a broad scope of interests. The closest comparison I can make is the time I was summoned for a jury pool in Dallas. Other than that, I cannot think of another mix of people more inherently different yet tasked to work together toward a common goal. In the classroom, students need to learn, and teachers need to engage the most challenging demographic one can be asked to reach. We are taking the most broad and eclectic mixture of hormonal, volatile, confused, challenged, athletic, brilliant, inexperienced, wonderful children, placing them all in the same room, and telling them to get along, learn algebra, finish their English papers, stay in their seats, be quiet, form groups, and turn off their phones.

The Stanky Leg

In 2008, the latest dance craze had just hit the Terrell, Texas scene. This was long before the dab, whip, and nae nae, but would have been just as big, if not bigger, had social media had the legs it does now. During a current events discussion, a student in my first-period class asked me if I knew about the "stanky leg." She provided a brief demonstration, for which she received bonus points and applause. As my students commenced Operation Derail the Teacher on a Fascinating Tangent, I was challenged by Destiny Williams to "do the stanky leg." As an uncertified first-year teacher, who had not yet had his coffee, I thought quickly and I made an offer they could not refuse. I proposed that if not just first period, but all class periods of Communication Applications passed the next test, I would hit the dance floor with the most incredible "stanky leg" possible.

Well, it worked. Sometimes the best motivator isn't grades, or discipline, but the strategic implementation of self-deprecation. I do not know how stanky my leg was, but judging by the handful of students rolling on the floor, it did not matter. All of my students passed, and no one was harmed during the making of my dance performance.

Superimposing the latest trends, phrases, viral videos, internet challenges, Netflix shows, and relatable content on top of your instruction and presentations is a simple way to promote student engagement. You can see their ears perk up, and questioning looks appear on their faces as you throw out a *"Haters gonna hate" a Taylor Swift, aka T-Swift song*. When you open the door for students to include their own interests, they are more likely to understand and provide additional, more relevant, valuable, and effective tools to enhance their learning and your instruction.

Design Through the Demographic

Video is an incredibly powerful and underutilized tool for teachers. From Pokemon to Spongebob, to Minecraft and Stranger Things, without the open student dialogue my approach fosters, I would have missed out on some of the best instructional resources that I use to this day. YouTube videos are their TV. Netflix is their cable. Video games and social media are part of their social livelihood.

There you will find the most relatable content and ways to reach, understand, appeal, and share with your demo.

Knowing your demo is the foundation for engaging your students in all aspects of teaching, instructional design, assessment, and technology integration. As you take the time implementing the curriculum, improving instruction, and enhancing your lesson plans, make sure that each and every step of the way you are relating, selling, and marketing to your demographic for an enhanced user experience. The more you know your students, the better your instruction can be designed to engage your students. Knowing your students is the ultimate goal, and when you do you will have completed the most important step in teaching like a DJ.

If Ryan Bingham's teacher had provided alternate instructional strategies to engage students' talents and passions, Ryan would not have failed. Exploring and learning the same content through Ryan's talents instead of through traditional means makes for better and more engaging instruction. Providing opportunities for students to demonstrate their understanding of the instructional goals by alternative means, utilizing their strengths and interests, will not only help reach the demographic but, most importantly, will enhance learning for all students.

A great teacher must know their demo, and find the best ways to reach the student before, during, and after instruction. The students must be at the forefront during all phases of planning curriculum, instruction, delivery, application, assessment, and lesson plans. The more you know your students, the more avenues will come to fruition to improve instruction and instructional design. Always keep your demo top of mind.

3 THE SHOW

"Don't reinvent the wheel, use a hoverboard."

I WAS STILL IN HIGH SCHOOL, but I might as well have been in Hollywood. It was my first time on the air by myself. Up until now, I had been on the air here and there as a guest and spent countless hours as a board operator for remote and sports broadcasts. Like a professional baseball player brought up from the minors, that Saturday morning from 10:00 a.m. to noon was my big shot to be the voice of the Dublin Saint Patrick's Day Parade.

It's not a televised event. Maybe in Dublin, Ireland—but not the one in Dublin, Texas—a small town of about four thousand people. The Dublin Bottling Works plant still makes its soda with real cane sugar. KCUB radio had a powerful signal in Dublin, and this was probably the only time I wished our signal was not so strong.

Every DJ has one of these moments and I have made plenty of

mistakes on the air. Most of the time, a mistake can be appreciated and realized as a moment to show some humility, and exude real personality as it happens live. The Dublin Saint Patrick's Day parade of '99 would prove to be my worst broadcast ever. Even my mother, to this day, will poke fun at me about the broadcast, and she is the sweetest person I know.

Russell Huffman, my program director trained me for the broadcast.

"I spoke with Norma (the station manager), and I convinced her that you are ready for this one. I need you to show up, read the sponsor names each break (on-air time designated for talk), and broadcast the parade from outside the Dublin Dr. Pepper Bottling Company."

Training complete. All training I received in my radio career would go this way. The ultimate "project-based instruction."

Looking back, I'm sure the real reason that I was given this broadcast "opportunity" was because Russell did not want to go in on Saturday. A wordsmith who also wrote for the Stephenville Empire-Tribune, he twisted words to make it more about me.

The only thing that could possibly have been "engaging" about my first broadcast was listening to one of the worst radio train wrecks in history. Not that broadcasting the Dublin St. Patrick's Day parade is ratings gold, or an event that draws interest from anyone not already participating in the parade, but my station manager could sell sponsorship to a grass-growing tournament. And, when she did, we would be there to cover the action.

My brother, Adam Mercer, was the board operator for this broadcast. He ran the controls, commercials, and music from the radio station. He realized in a hurry that I was in trouble. He began to help me as I was drowning in radio waves. He figured out a way to speak to me while I was live on the air so only I could hear. "What type of cars? What colors? What are people doing? Why should I go there?" he nudged me. Anything he could think of to make this broadcast more engaging and save me from further embarrassment to the family name.

The following Monday, I showed up to work like an athlete showing up for film review after a big loss. My program director said that it seemed I might have struggled with my broadcast and finally gave me some helpful tips, "Get the *Stephenville Empire-Tribune*. All of the day's events and activities are there on a timeline, and by the time you split it up over your breaks, you will have more than enough information. Interviewing the sponsors, community leaders, and business owners is also good practice and very important." Thanks, boss.

You must be better prepared, and know how to design your show. When you turn the mic on, you must always have a plan. Teachers are "live" every day. Winging it on-air can lead to bad radio. Winging it in the classroom leads to discipline problems, and bad teaching.

It is always easier to cut material than to search for it during a live broadcast. Every on-air break needs twice the material necessary for the length of the break. If you are interviewing a guest to fill the time, prepare twice the number of questions you think will be necessary. If you are playing a game, prepare backup games, extra questions, and have emergency prizes ready. Trying to resolve any content issue by finding material on-air keeps you from focusing on making the live moments as fun and entertaining. Make every second count.

Make it appeal to the audience, and present it in a way to engage the listeners, even if the content is the farthest thing from entertaining. Sometimes, the event or information is boring. I needed to know how to prepare for specific events, broadcasts, or whenever the mic was on!

Every time the broadcast started, and the mic was on, I would have a purpose and goal of engaging our audience and keeping them tuned in to the show. When I turned off the mic, I wanted the audience to have experienced the content by speaking live on the air. A message would be delivered. An introduction, significant content, and conclusion or call to action would be provided. I did not talk just to fill time. Speak with a purpose and the audience will appreciate the consideration of their time. The Show is your instructional design in the classroom, and every part of your instruction should be designed to teach like a DJ.

What's Your Secret?

I was in part inspired by a staff development workshop presented by Dexter Dumas. It took place just before school started my first year. He was electric, passionate, and eccentric. I would be reporting directly to him, so I went to greet him after his presentation. I appreciated the passion he had for his job, and I wanted to ask him about his own inspirations.

I approached and asked Mr. Dumas, "Hey, what's your secret?"

"Just keep them engaged," was his response.

I think he misunderstood me. He knew I was a new teacher, and thought I was asking how to approach my first year that was just four days away. I expected him to say his secret was coffee, daily exercise, or a gluten-free diet. But no, he said, "Just keep them *engaged*." In a word—the lifeblood of a radio show, a radio DJ, a radio station. That is what I had trained for every day during my radio career. Immediately, I felt relief and excitement.

"I can do that!" I thought to myself. At least here I am not competing with Kidd Kraddick. Now, I will have five, forty-nine minute shows. Athletics during one period, where I would be told what to teach. Sounds like a five-hour show to me, and with this show, we can reuse the same content over and over. The last show ought to be really good!

Five minutes before show time on the first day of school, I actually thought to myself ... *What have I done?* The audience was filing in the room. Less than a month ago, I had been paid three hundred and fifty dollars to show up at a mall and give away prizes. People actually wanted to meet me in person, and sometimes even asked for an autograph. I had no idea if my instructional design would even work. Just surviving to my lunch break seemed a feasible goal.

Well, they showed up. They always do. Every day you are live and you better be prepared. I was prepared-ish. I was also coaching my first year. This meant my first day was July 21 and I would work Monday through Saturday until the first day of school, and then seven days a week through November. I was also uncertified, so I was completing online courses during any free time.

Thank goodness Galen Rosenberg, the other Speech teacher, provided me with his PowerPoints a few days earlier, or I may not have survived. Well, regardless of ready or not, resources or not, tired or not, seven days a week or not, first time or not, we were live. I was a teacher.

Thirty seconds into the live classroom show, it happened. My audience laughed, they smiled, they didn't seem to hate me. The room wasn't spontaneously erupting in fights and make-out sessions. I thought to work in radio was the best job in the world, but that day I realized that I was wrong and now I really had the best job in the world: Classroom Teacher.

Instructional Design

I already had a plan of attack for how to teach Speech my first semester. It was years in the making. As a student, I would pick apart my teacher's instruction and imagine ways I could present better. To begin my first official instructional design I took the best parts of every speech class from junior high through college and designed the best speech class possible. Almost everything I could remember was a real project, presentation, or game, like numerous impromptu games during Mrs. Crain's Speech class, writing songs in Mrs. Wesson's class, making movies in Mrs. Campbell-Furtick's class, and special instructional delivery like Señor Muniz singing instructional Spanish songs he had written on his guitar (and that I can still sing today). After the foundation was set and I learned that my instructional design was working well, my new goal would be to make improvements and adjustments to redesign the instruction every semester: ensuring that it would be the best.

"The textbook may be old, but the instruction needs to be fresh!"
I knew where to start as a Speech teacher: with the fundamentals and the best parts of every Speech class I had taken in school and college. At the time, Speech class was referred to as Communication Applications and later changed to Professional Communication. It just so happened that the textbook for the class was the same one from my high school (and ten years old). The best part, and the difference maker for me, was the ability to take the old content and deliver it in new and engaging ways, like I had practiced for so long on the radio. After Mr. Rosenberg provided the instructional material, the rest was fun. I could begin putting the show together.

I also knew that I needed the material to be presented and integrated in a way that would ensure learning at a high level. To do this, we would need all lessons to have a hands-on component, but also include auditory, visual, and kinesthetic elements. And, most importantly, a little "something extra" to motivate and inspire. Students will step up when provided with a challenge and a chance to do something new, special, different, or meaningful. Tip: Do not limit the project or assessment with expectations. Expectations should just be a standard to be broken every time.

I wanted to create learning experiences. Experiences that drew on all five senses. Experiences that included the most current research and information. Technology would be utilized to design, create, produce, provide, share, analyze, and assess the instruction, student learning, and to engage students.

Instruction is most effective when all learning styles are accommodated during every part of instruction. Not just because some learn one way and some another, but because exposure to multiple resources along the way ensures an even better understanding of the material and encourages students to work together. I want the learning experience to involve audio, visual, and kinesthetic activities that must be explored to reach the instructional goal. Ideally, by the time the project is complete, the student has minimally reached the instructional goal through the process, but potentially has discovered more above and beyond the original instructional goal.

A Gifted and Talented test in 6th grade did not produce the

results I anticipated. I couldn't figure out which way the gears would turn as it lay there on the page as a two-dimensional image—but I still believed I was gifted. Mrs. Wesson recognized my talent and realized that I learned another way. I was even told over and over that I was not mechanically inclined and that I was a visual learner. I do not like this! Do not put your students in a box, and do not tell a student they are a certain way, learn a certain way, and have any limitations due to some preconceived notions.

In today's world, I am able to learn my way. I do much better teaching myself than in any course of instruction. When a teacher or professor hoards the information, relying solely on a textbook or lecture instruction, it is just not good for me. Working my way, I have learned to restore a DeLorean, speak Spanish, write this book, teach fourteen different courses for grades six through twelve, and facilitate teachers—and that's just in the past five years!

Make every course, unit, or lesson a mission, goal, or journey. Give the instruction a real purpose. Now, a version of this idea is called "gamifying," or making each lesson a game. When I started teaching, I just wanted to use different and more motivational language to stand out from the other teachers and modes of instruction. I would much rather complete a quest, journey, or operation than an assignment or test.

Don't teach me something I can watch on YouTube. Teach me through the process, exploration, and discovery. Let's discover the material as it was discovered the first time. Let's recreate real-life situations that ensure the material is covered and lived. As we complete the journey or reach our goal, the material is discovered naturally, and therefore allows real learning to occur.

"It's the climb." —Miley Cyrus

Even if the project or product is not pretty at the end, learning occurred during the process, and that learning is the goal—the real part of the experience to assess. When the journey is over and your student sees the scoreboard, as long as they made the trip and survived the experience, they will have won.

Kids today are bombarded by so much stimuli. If you wanna compete, you gotta attack. Keep it coming. Keep it changing. Forget format and structure. Keep the students on their toes. They should not know what hit them. Attack at all angles. You can hear the instruction, watch it, rewind it, examine examples, collaborate, share, inspire, motivate, and live the instructional experience that takes place with the student in the classroom, outside of class, in the community, and beyond.

A good show in the classroom is going to be real, reliable, relatable, open, challenging, witty, smart, silly, fun, entertaining, and educational. My first few years as a Communication Applications teacher, I talked through half of each period. I liked it. It reminded me of being on the radio. I would get their attention, and then we would do an activity related to the instructional goal. Finally, we would practice, drill, or play, utilizing the new instructional material via new technology, games, or various hands-on, real-world activities.

Later, my instructional design would evolve into hardly speaking at all and simply facilitating the instruction, activities, and projects as learning goals were discovered. I would be free to move around the room and experience the learning with the students individually, in groups, or all together. Either method works, if you set up your instructional design effectively. You and your students will have more freedom to engage, explore, and discover.

I did not want to become the teacher that was teaching how things used to be done. I had a professor in college that taught me about radio from an outdated textbook. If it is going to be good instruction, it has to be real and current. It is more challenging to design instruction that is the most current and there are not always instructions or instructional resources available. You do it live. You may mess up and the project may not work well, but it will always be better because it is real. Take chances, challenge yourself, and know that mistakes may be made along the way, but learning will always occur.

As a Communication Applications teacher and Debate coach at Frisco High School, I would use all the new technology possible. I believed that my responsibility to prepare my students for the future meant that new technology must be used effectively and as often as possible. Students would need to be able to communicate effectively and professionally with whatever devices were available. Our debate team would be the first to be one-hundred percent paperless. I have not used a piece of paper for instruction since 2010. I did use some poster board one time to draw up battle plans to inspire a big project. It worked.

All my presentations are upgraded and enhanced with the best presentation tools possible. Every assignment, project, and presentation by the students utilize only the most current and innovative tools. Everything for my classes is available online: all resources, notes, instructions, lesson audio, video, and tutorials. Students collaborate and share seamlessly to enhance instruction. My students engage with my instruction and affect their own self-discovery. Classwork is project-based and I am able to witness and cheer them on as it happens. Learning experiences occur live in the classroom. The instruction and projects help students understand the instructional goals at a high level. It's fun, and real learning occurs!

I once heard that teachers should re-evaluate and update their instruction every three years. I do it daily, constantly, all the time. I want to use the most recent research, technology, and methods. No two courses are ever taught verbatim. It is much more work, but way more fun and beneficial for all. If you are not challenging yourself and your students with the most current information, technology, and tools, then you are not designing the best instruction. Be the best, and be the first. The students will like the challenge and will rise to it.

4 SHOW PREP

"The best projects are made using instructions that are not yet written."

THE SHOW PREP is your lesson plan. To ensure your listening audience will have quality content for the entire show, the show prep is essential. Show prep is one of the most important steps to teach like a DJ.

Since the end of the last show, a keen eye and a close-to-the-ground ear have been gathering potential demographic-related show material and content. The show is now packed, relevant, and purposeful for every scheduled on-air break. Every break is pre-planned to provide varied content, including diverse topics, interviews, bits, stunts, live music, listener interaction, and games. Research and materials are consolidated for the most relevant news, sports, weather, and traffic updates. Social media, live streams, and multimedia are produced and ready to air and upload online. Throughout the entire process, strategic scrutinizing lets the DJ adjust the content to keep the listeners tuned-in to the show. The show in its entirety is now ready to air.

You can show prep all day to produce the best show. Your content is ever-changing as news and information can change and be shared so quickly. That is the best approach because in the worst-case scenario, you have a full show planned at the highest level of engagement for your demo. In my very best shows and most of my favorite shows, I didn't even use the majority of the prep. The best radio shows come together when real life, real experiences, and genuine personalities are evident as the show broadcasts. Real reactions, feelings, and an opportunity to genuinely know the DJ's, guests, and listeners occurs. You need the show prep material, because it sparks even better topics and content, and gives you a fallback when the conversation lags. Anticipating a real moment or opportunity to explore on the air (versus a pre-planned, scripted bit) is a skill. It is often more work, but always better radio.

The daily show prep for a DJ entails finding the most relevant content for the various show parts, games, bits, news, interviews, intro, close, and content before the show. During the show, and after, show prep still occurs as you continuously look for the best material and plan creative ways to present that material. Pop culture, news, sports, breaks, and games all require time and energy spent researching and producing.

During show prep, you go through each break and plan how and what will be provided for your audience. To teach like a DJ, the same mindset is necessary for lesson plan design. Working to find the most relevant and current instructional content, and presenting said instruction in the most engaging ways to your students is essential. The best content can (and often will) change as the show is happening live. In the classroom, students may find better and more efficient ways to learn during instruction that can benefit their learning and the rest of the class.

I'm No Ryan Seacrest

American Idol was still a relevant discussion topic in 2007, especially since that season's auditions would include a stop in Dallas. I was tasked with reporting live from the *American Idol* auditions at Texas Stadium. I would broadcast live from the event to paint the scene and share the excitement with our listeners.

I did not like being outside of the studio during the show, as all of the behind-the-scenes production work would still be waiting for me when I returned to the station, keeping me at work later than usual. My only consolation was that at least on this trip, someone else (the singer trying out) was more likely to look like an idiot than me—which I usually did when broadcasting outside the studio.

Not much happens at the *American Idol* auditions other than waiting. I knew there would be some crazy attention-seekers in attendance. I thought about even holding some auditions of my own as they waited in line, to get a feel for that year's talent. It was fun just finding out where the thousands of hopefuls came from, and how long they had been waiting. It was also worthwhile describing what was going on behind the scenes of the *American Idol* process, as the producers, film crews, boom mics, and cameras scurried around and through the audience for extra B-roll footage for the new season, still several months away.

I needed what people in the radio business call "radio gold," and I was running out of time. I had not found the next Kelly Clarkson waiting in line. I wanted a break that was so good, I could call it a wrap and head back to the station in victory. The celebrity judges were not there yet, as in this early round the show's producers were responsible for narrowing the field of thousands to a few hundred. I would not get to kick it with Paula, Simon, or my dawg Randy.

Suddenly, it happened. A producer's dream. Like a glorious unicorn leaping out of a forest into an open field, shining a brilliant beam of light from its magical horn, a celebrity appeared. I knew her, too. Well, not personally—but I did watch her entire season when she was on *American Idol*. And, recently, by chance, I had even watched her new TV show—the very show that she was currently filming at this moment. She was fully equipped with an entire crew of producers, staff, and videographers. Contestants huddled around her every step of the way. She got way more attention than me and my cell phone. I had a squad of one, but I was determined to get her on the air with us. Then I could return to the station a hero, and make it rain "radio gold."

Carrie Underwood won *American Idol* Season 4 in 2005. Actually, she has had so much success since then that most people may not even remember that *American Idol* launched her career. Carrie was still relevant too—dating Tony Romo, and her music all over the radio. By that point, she had already started accumulating Country Music Awards and Grammys.

I called back to the station to find out how soon we could go live and to let the others know that we would be interviewing Carrie Underwood. I still had to get over there, break through her entourage, and find out if she would even do the interview. But, I was confident: this was going to happen. She seemed nice enough when I watched her show. The next live break was less than five minutes away.

"Make way, coming through, excuse me, pardon me, Mix 102.9 here ..."

Finally, she took a break from her own teleprompted recording, backdropped by of a sea of potential *Idol* contestants. I swooped right in and asked if she wouldn't mind going live with me on Mix 102.9 to talk about what she was currently up to with her show and her music. She said yes. I knew we would be live in a couple of minutes and she said that would be fine. Perfect!

One thing several DJs do (and may seem bizarre at first) is to not speak about on-air content during the breaks. If you know something is going to be asked, shared, or discussed on the show, you don't want to waste the first reaction. Personal stories, show topics, celebrity gossip, and life-changing situations shared between the hosts and listeners are aired live. The same applies to guests on the show, and the questions that will be posed. "Save it for the show," is what we say. You are guaranteed to receive the most genuine reactions and responses if you wait until the mics are on.

I always did it that way, but looking back, I would have been better off in the mindset of a "producer," versus that of a DJ. A producer will dot the I's and cross the t's, acquiring questions, details, names, credentials, and information prior to the show to omit the chance for any embarrassment. DJs spend the countdown to going live in silence, reviewing material, or in meaningless banter and chit chat as we save the real content for the next live break in 3, 2, 1 ...

> *"I am so excited to surprise you guys with a big-time celebrity that I found here at the American Idol auditions. To everyone back at the station, and to all of you wonderful listeners it is with great pleasure this morning that I welcome to the show the beautiful and amazing Carrie Underwood."*

I pass the cell phone over. My job is done. If we had a remote, live broadcasting setup, I would be responsible for providing questions and banter with the celebrity guest. Since we only had time to bring my cell phone this morning, the hosts back at the station would handle it until the end of the interview, and then I would close the break out when the phone was handed back to me, so we would not be passing the cellphone back and forth throughout the interview. Typically, they would say their hellos, field some questions from the hosts, and appropriately follow up or adjust depending on the responses from the celebrity. But that's not how it went this time. The cell phone situation was now the least of my worries.

At the very moment that I said the name "Carrie Underwood" out loud, relinquishing the phone into her hand and looking directly into the eyes of this beautiful celebrity TV show host that I previously and appropriately described as a "frolicking unicorn," I realized my mistake. Her gleaming smile shifted first to confusion, then to shock.

I had indeed watched her on *American Idol* Season 4. I had even watched her fancy new TV show just a few weeks prior. But it was too late. The damage was done. She had the mic. I was speechless. It was not Carrie Underwood, the number one artist of the year.

"Um, it's Kimberly Caldwell," she responded. Chaos ensued, because trust me, there was nothing else happening in front of the 10,000 auditioners waiting in line. We were the only entertainment. Her film crew surrounded us, with an entourage of producers and staff. I had just made this announcement live on the radio for an audience of (potentially) fifty thousand listeners. The

American Idol film crew and its big remote-control-crowd-camera perched above us, spying on anything that might be entertaining. I am only assuming the other Morning Mix hosts were laughing just as hysterically as everyone else in my vicinity. I tried to explain that I knew who she was, that I knew she was Kimberly Caldwell—but no one cared, and there was nothing more I could do. I just sat myself down on a curb in the parking lot of Texas Stadium, shaking my head in disbelief, as this played itself out on-air.

In my defense, Kimberly placed 4th in 2005 on *American Idol*. But no doubt it was salt in the wound for Kimberly, because not only did I get her name wrong in front of thousands and three different vessels of mass communication, but Carrie Underwood was Kimberly's toughest competition and the ultimate winner of *American Idol* that season.

In the haze of the aftermath, I remember Kimberly Caldwell kicking me in the butt a few times on the air, for all to see and hear. She was justifiably joined by the rest of the Morning Mix crew. Several callers followed who thought their opinions should be aired as well. One caller even asked where to send in his resume for the new morning show producer position that would certainly be available.

I apologized to Kimberly several times, and she said not to worry; she was very kind once we were off the air. The last thing I remember was her producer, who stood by my side throughout this fiasco, leaning over to me and in almost a whisper saying, "Wow, that was embarrassing."

Later, upon arrival at the radio station, I was embarrassed (and I do not embarrass easily). Surprisingly, and to my dismay, Rick O'Bryan, my boss and program director, thought it was absolutely radio gold.

"Hey, did you do that on purpose?" he asked.
"Because that was great, just great. You should do that every time you go out of the studio. Just play dumb, and mess up people's names, and things like that. Just mess things up everywhere you go."

He was right. When done purposely, it is a creative and well-produced bit that one might be proud to take credit for and celebrate. By accident, it is just plain embarrassing.

The best and most memorable radio shows are the ones when you are directed away from your plan and follow a more significant or relevant tangent as it unfurls. When you recognize a new avenue to engage that is more real and meaningful to your students it will be more engaging and always better, even without having tested the new idea. Lesson plans are made to be broken. You cannot be scared to leave the comfort of your original plan, script, or ideas. You can't be lazy at this moment either. The new way will always be more work and more challenging, but the benefits are always worth the effort and provide the greatest results and real learning experiences.

Every Second Counts

I was producing a morning show, screening calls, and mid-game for a chance to win fabulous tickets to see Taylor Swift, when Senator John McCain called in for his phone interview. We were running behind. The game would not be over for two more minutes, we needed to find a winner on another line, commercials had to follow, and I needed to keep Senator McCain entertained so he would stay on the line for the interview we had promoted all morning.

It was handled. Nothing a little political banter couldn't solve. McCain stayed occupied, ecstatic winners were headed to Taylor Swift, and the show aired seamlessly to the listening audience. I would buy some Tums on the way home.

Every day, show prep is done for every good radio show. Bookmarked sites across the internet are scoured. Show prep services collate all forms of material to share with the audience. Current events, 'this day in history,' celebrity birthdays, weird news, celebrity news, bit ideas, phone topics, pop culture news, and games are made available through these services. Then, the DJ or producer will cull, screen, and determine the best material for the show. Each break or moment on the air that is not music or commercials is populated by daily and weekly segments for the entire length of the show.

Every hour, every bit, every second of air-time is accounted for during a radio show. The same should hold true when teaching like a DJ. Do not waste the students' time. When you talk, have a purpose. Get after it from bell to bell. No busy work—just real work.

If they are good, teachers have lesson plans prepared for the entire class period every day of instruction. Articles, books, videos, audio, worksheets, activities, guest speakers, assessments, and websites are scoured, sorted, posted, and presented to engage students at the highest level for the length of the class period. Making every second count, and ensuring that the audience is engaged, tuned in, and wanting more every step of the way.

Big Walk Through

An Instructional Technology facilitator from Frisco High School called me and said that some school administrators from other districts would be touring two campuses in our district, and observing two classes. She wanted my class to be one of the observations and asked if I could put together a lesson that demonstrated our usage of new instructional technology.

Her request was much easier than most would anticipate since this was how our class ran. A lesson plan was already made, as every day we approached learning the same way. It did not matter when the other school districts would stop by; we would be doing our thing, and they would be welcome to join in on the fun.

They timed the visit to coincide with the start of class, which was nice. That way, the visitors would know what was going on and would not think that the students have just taken over the classroom. Devices and phones are on, students in their own groups, inside and outside the classroom, and the teacher seemingly just walking around. What I did not anticipate was the powerful presence of about fifteen individuals in suits simultaneously walking into the classroom, forming a semicircle along the back of the room, like some sort of FBI raid. I was fine—I love an audience—but my kids had a look of fear.

It took a little bit longer than normal to get the students fired up. The way we communicated and learned in that class could be a little chaotic to outsiders. The kids instinctively did not want to jump in as intensely as normal with all of our scary guests in the back of the room.

We stuck to the lesson plan. The kids ended up attacking the activity like trained professionals. It was a wonderful lesson. The kids did so well and were so engaged, I was able to spend most of the time speaking with the visitors about the wonderful things our kids were learning and creating. No one even knew it at the time, but my amazing student aide Monika Adel was in that class. She decided to actually do the activity, because as she told me at the time, "It just seemed like so much fun." One of the groups in the hallway sitting on the floor against the lockers had a student named Anna Jagneaux. She didn't speak a whole lot back then, but I remember vividly the day she said, "I like learning this way (using Google Docs and online tools to research, complete, and turn in projects). It gives me more control."

TLADJ Lesson Plan

Start with the instructional goal. Explore the instruction through the most current, relevant, and engaging audio, video, and kinesthetic means to reach the goal. If we start with the instructional goal and design the best way to reach the goal through engaging instruction, the student will reach the goal and beyond. Focus on the big picture, and the real-world stuff. Make it real. Recreate the discovery. Make it a challenge. Make it fun. The learning occurs in the process—not the lesson, instruction, or product.

Objective:

At Frisco High School the objective for the lesson had to be clearly written each day on the top right corner of the whiteboard. The thinking was that if students know what they will be learning about before they learn it, they will learn it better. I liked this idea, but it would be the reason for my first trip to the assistant principal's office.

It would not be my last trip to the principal's office. Not even my last trip to Mr. Antwine's office (an Assistant Principal at Frisco High School tasked with providing random walk-throughs of the classrooms and sharing feedback). One day, during Mr. Antwine's walk-through, my objective was covered up by the projector screen. We were not using a book; the links and tools we were using were being projected because all of the instruction was digital. But, Mr. Antwine was right. He walked in our room. He approached a student and asked what we were doing that day. She said she did not know.

I remember witnessing this occurrence. I knew that Mr. Antwine was going to ask a student what the objective was as he made his way over to one. She was a freshman, and in my head I was thinking, "Please don't ask her," because she looked so scared. She was like a little baby deer, and here comes this big fancy suited man as we are just making ourselves comfortable in class. But, regardless, I needed to do better. I vowed that from that day forward, not a day would go by where a student did not know the objective. I would channel all of my radio show intro techniques. By whatever means necessary … it was on. Challenge accepted!

I bought a ukulele, several kazoos, a vuvuzela, slingshot-screaming monkeys, guitars, a gong, bongos, costumes, and megaphones (handheld and fanny pack style). I introduced technological advances including but not limited to a DJ booth, amplifiers, a sound effects board, microphones, and a scrolling marquee. Imagine, a scrolling marquee just broadcasting the day's objective, over and over. I would even add secret messages and hidden opportunities for bonus points as the scrolling marquee had no limit to the amount of content it could hold. It is still funny to this day to listen to the class read the scrolling messages, like robots in unison.

I still found that students did not always read the objective, scrolling or not. So, sometimes it was necessary to begin singing the objective, interpretive dancing the objective, or rapping the objective. Or, just to go freestyle with the bongos. I updated my app game with some of the greatest to this day like the T-Pain app, AutoRap, Talking Tom, and the Lightsaber app. Now the class introduction, during which I set the objective and instructional goals, is one of my favorite parts of any lesson.

Not only did I write the objective in the top right corner of the whiteboard under big blue stickers provided by the school that read "OBJECTIVE," but I turned it into an "I Can ... statement." The "I Can..." statement clearly expresses what the student would be able to do with the new knowledge after the lesson—a good way to make the objective seem real and relevant. A real-world skill would be possible when the lesson was complete.

We experienced the objective-statement and plan. Every student read it, sang it, danced it, or rapped it. My objective and goals would also be scrolling in the space above the projector screen, in a continuous marquee of instructional greatness for all to see.

Warm-Up:

"We need to warm up our brain muscles and get after it today. You do not want to pull a brain muscle, and today there is a chance of having your mind blown two or three times, so please warm up today."

Some teachers call this a "bell ringer" activity. I try not to use any terminology that all other teachers use, as I like to stand out and it helps to engage the students. I do like the "warm-up" term, as if class is a sporting event and we need to get ready.

I often use the warm-up to reiterate the objective and to check prior knowledge that is necessary for the new instructional goal. In Speech classes, we may write and act out some topical skits. In audio and video production classes we may plan production for timely, current event projects, or find the best examples to share of new video ideas to produce. Many of these can be shared with devices, computers, and through the teacher's projector as they are discussed in the first ten to fifteen minutes of instruction. If we are mid-project, I prefer letting the students jump right into their projects. When the students are that motivated, your instruction is on point. Sometimes the warm-up activity is getting to continue designing your incredible creation.

Activity:

The activity will be something that insists a student learn the instructional goal. It can be accomplished in one class or over several, but in the end, when the student has completed the activity, project, presentation, or assessment, the learning has already occurred. The best radio is real radio, and the best lessons are real lessons. No busy work. When real work is occurring, learning happens.

The instruction includes audio, video, and kinesthetic opportunities and resources shared throughout the class. I do not care how the students learn best (and some may need all types of instructional materials) because all are provided and available. Be flexible and plentiful with instruction resources. Always provide options, and celebrate exploration with applications, technology, or other means of exploring and discovering the instructional goal. Proving time to become familiar with the app or tool will lead to better projects and more fun completing the projects.

I will have a base plan for the activity, and tools to use, but like listeners calling into the radio show, students often have better ideas. I will give students their own control and freedom. Be flexible with the product as well. I have had students who were really good artists so we compromised on a project where they used Photoshop or a web-based drawing app. A gamer may want to make a game. A musician may want to make a music video. Let it happen—these are often the best artifacts for future instructional resources and often lead to better instructional strategies.

I tell the students not to rush. You can't force a genius idea. If they have time to think of an idea or theme they are interested in, they always go above and beyond with the product. I will allocate time just to think about it, even an entire class period to share ideas and dream big until they get their idea for their project that they will work twice as hard complete.

Tools:

Apps, computers, devices, or anything the students may need to use before, during, or after the lesson. Time to turn on, set up, or prepare devices can be allocated during the warm-up time. Lesson planning is an appropriate time for the teacher to test to make sure the technology will work appropriately. I ask my student aides to test all future instructional or web-based tools before the lesson. Always give time for students to explore a tool if it is new. This will pay off in the long run with better examples and projects, as students will have more fun pushing themselves to utilize the new instructional tool. Students will have a better understanding of the new tool and be able to use it in the future for other projects and teachers.

Resources:

Resources include websites, links, notes, books, audio, video, or any other instructional resources that will help the student discover the material. I provide all instructional resources on our class website: a one-stop shop for students, it ensures all forms of learning instruction are available. Students can read it, watch it, or hear it, and all will end up living it and teaching it by the time the lesson is complete.

Wrap Up:

Projects can be assessed as they are created. Really, all students should get a 100% grade as the teacher is available to ensure the learning is occurring as it happens. Students can share and critique digitally to save time. By the time all of the students have shared their projects, there should not be a student in the class who doesn't understand the material inside and out due to the multitude of different examples. As the projects are completed, they can be shared or presented. Another sharing opportunity is available during the warm-up time the next day. Or, my favorite, and discussed later, is a grand event where all creations are celebrated and shared.

Instructional Timeline:

Depending on the length of the class period and if you have block scheduling, lessons can be spread across class periods or even weeks if necessary. Sometimes I will have students cover an entire unit this way. We use a day to prep and warm up, a week to investigate, discover, learn, and share, and then a full day to present and reflect. Just like lesson plans are made to be broken, so are timelines. If you or your students have a better idea and need to move on, feel free! Need more time exploring? Take it! You can't beat when real learning is occurring, and the students are making it happen.

Allow students to explore the material through their passions and interests. Recreate the real world experiences that led to the discoveries. Provide multiple means and methods to learn, explore, and discover. Students are bombarded with images, videos, audio, memes, music, and media. Bombard them right back as you incorporate all forms of media with and throughout your instruction, tools, resources, and presentations.

Redesign all of your instructional tools, resources, materials, slide shows, and forms of media to be the most relevant, professional, engaging, and entertaining. If you are bored during instruction, they are bored, and boredom leads to discipline problems and angry teachers. Save a teacher, eradicate boredom. If you take the time to design the best instruction, you will have almost an entire class period to facilitate the learning, to ensure they are on the right track, to cheer them on, and to motivate them to go further as you watch the learning occur live in the classroom.

5 THE STUDIO

"You can always tell a good radio show by how messy the studio is at the end. The same rule applies in the classroom."

I THINK A CLASSROOM should look like a cross between Willy Wonka's Chocolate Factory and NASA. Your classroom environment is just as important as your instructional design. A bad environment will significantly hurt the potential for learning. A great classroom environment will elevate learning to a higher level. To teach like a DJ, make your studio your classroom. This is where the magic happens!

Do Not Make Direct Eye Contact With James Blunt
We had just finished our live interview with James Blunt when I asked him if he wouldn't mind recording a few liners with me before starting a live show next door in the Full Throttle Garage. (A liner is a short recording that plays between songs to promote the show or radio station.) He was happy to oblige, and when we

finished he asked if I was going to go next door to watch his performance. I really did not want to go. I was so tired of his song. "You're Beautiful" had run on the radio for what seemed like four years straight. But I was trapped. I knew it. There was no way out of this one. When James Blunt asks if you will watch him perform a free show in a room so close to your studio that you actually share a wall, you say, "Of course I'm going." After all, he'd just taken time out of his day to record liners for the show. It meant I would once again be taken away from my studio, and I would have another late day at the office.

My production studio was wedged between the Mix 102.9 studio and the Full Throttle Garage. The single window in my studio looked straight into the on-air studio, abutting the control board and computer screens. The Full Throttle Garage was to my right, parallel to our on-air and production studios. The window blinds could be opened to catch any live event hosted by any of the seven other iHeartRadio stations on the same floor.

Upon walking into the iHeartRadio floor, there were listener and guest lounges with huge flat screen TVs, indoor billboards, leather chairs, and sofas. A real modern look: classy and shiny. Tours for friends, family, and students featured the on-air and production studios, including framed and mounted posters, photos, and autographs from the celebrities and musicians who were hot at the time. A swing by the Total Traffic Network (a hub for radio traffic reporting throughout Texas) just before a look at the radio signal processors was just as fascinating. You could see most of the technology necessary to host and send analog and digital signals for seven radio stations, and at least as many production studios.

The studio and production room was state-of-the-art and brand new. When I started in Dallas, they had just completed renovation. They took over an entire floor of the Clear Channel building, installing the latest and greatest digital broadcast equipment for the DJs, producers, and production staff. It occupied the third-floor corner suite that overlooked the Dallas North Tollway and the Galleria—an area of Dallas where I would spend plenty of time embarrassing myself and harassing nearby businesses by dancing, singing, and conducting other ridiculous forms of costume-based performances.

My production studio was much the same, with more technology for audio, video, and web production. It was similar to Doc Brown's lab from *Back to the Future,* due to the audio and video recording and editing equipment throughout the studio. It was darker, with a couch and chair for guests. The production room alone was worth more money than all of the equipment at my previous radio stations combined. Entrance to the Full Throttle Garage was behind my production studio. Don't let the "Garage" in the name of this sponsored studio fool you. This place was fancy and sleek. It felt like entering the Willy Wonka Chocolate Factory, but instead of delicious treats, there were plush couches, chairs, and rugs. There were professional backdrops and live performance and broadcast equipment for entertainers. Small crowds of about twenty fans or so could win their chance to be in the audience for a half-hour show, interview, meet & greet, and photo. Several employees might sneak their way in too, depending on their celebrity preferences. I do remember quite a long line of ladies when Dwayne (The Rock) Johnson was there.

I likewise remember watching Natasha Bedingfield dancing on the huge fluffy couch, and then swan-diving onto the oversized bean bag. It was just so inviting. Classy, yet fun. Professional, yet cool. Simple and amazing. This setup would inspire my future classroom design.

For the James Blunt performance, I sat in the back next to the producer. The place was full, but all were comfy, and all would have a great view. James started his first song. It was not "You're Beautiful," but a song I'd never heard. (To be fair, I didn't know any other James Blunt music.) James was strumming his guitar like Charlie Daniels' fiddle player. It was simple and complex at the same time. It was just James, his acoustic, and the resonance of a passionate, elegant, and strong tone. The chorus came along and this song "1973" immediately became one of my favorites.

James was on fire. He delivered the bridge, followed again by the chorus, and his passion was infectious as he stared out over the crowd. We were a part of this performance. Suddenly and without warning, it happened. James Blunt, nearing the final verse of the song, tracked me down with his eyes and locked in. As if he knew I had reservations. As if he knew that I had made fun of the song played so many times on what seemed like every radio station. As if he knew that I was more of a hard-rock and hip-hop guy. His eyes were powerful and magical, and in that moment I was overwhelmed by my first "man crush." I downloaded his entire collection as soon as I got home that day. It had everything to do with the atmosphere created in that room—a place where it felt like anything was possible.

Even working in radio market number 242 in the country, at Kicker 107 in Abilene, Texas, the appearance of the station, the studio, the vehicles, and the equipment was a priority. The hallways were decorated with poster-sized portraits of the most relevant country artists at the time. The studios were freshly painted, the station van had a fresh new wrap, and all equipment was new. Every guest that stopped by was offered a tour and given some free swag from the prize closet.

I want my classroom to send the same message. Students should want to be in my room. They should feel comfortable, welcome, relaxed and inspired. The layout even coerces students in to hanging out and "belonging" in the front of the room, so when asked to give speeches they already feel more comfortable. It has the latest and greatest technology. It looks like Willy Wonka met NASA.

A New Challenge

After I left radio, I had about a month to find a teaching job. It was July of 2008. *This has to be easier than finding radio jobs*, I thought. I spoke with some of my favorite coaches, principals, and former teachers to see what I needed to do to make it happen. I had a degree in Communications and a minor in Computer Information Technology. I learned that I could be emergency-certified to teach Communication Applications. My Speech teachers (Diana Hassler, and Sherry Crain) and their courses were the reason I wanted to become a teacher, the reason I became a DJ, and the reason I studied Communications in college. If I was not going to DJ, I was going to be a Speech teacher. It had always been my fallback plan, and before radio, my goal. I would sit through every class I ever took thinking of ways to make this class better.

Turns out that finding a Speech teaching gig is not much easier than finding your own radio show. There were a grand total of three Speech openings in Texas. I could teach Speech and coach varsity football and junior varsity soccer at Terrell High School in Terrell, Texas, or teach Speech and coach varsity football and junior varsity soccer at Lumberton High School in Lumberton, Texas just north of Beaumont. The other Speech position was south of Dallas, in Red Oak, and had no coaching component, but they missed out on the chance to hire an uncertified first-year teacher by never responding.

I was offered both jobs. I know how to conduct myself during a job interview. I should, as it is part of the Speech curriculum. I actually believed that during both of these campus visits I really just had to not mess up the interview and the job would be mine, despite my lack of instructional credentials. You see, I had an ace in the hole: my football career was every bit as extensive as my radio experience. From where I was living in Dallas, Terrell was only twenty minutes away. Plus they paid $20,000 more per year than Lumberton, so the decision was easy.

Surprise! Welcome to the coaching profession. The job started in one week. Evidently, even new-hire coaches work through the summer and I would start the following Monday (July 21). We had fields to prepare, equipment rooms to paint, and summer workouts to run. It would have been nice to have had the time to work on my online certification. Instead, I fit my online courses in between the five Speech classes I taught that first year and seven-days-a-week varsity football—a long season that bled right into soccer practices. My last radio paycheck was in June, and I did not receive a paycheck from the school until September 25. Keep this tidbit in mind as my story continues.

At the start of the school year, my classroom was abysmal. Old white brick walls like a psychiatric ward. I had big ideas for this place, and a very blank canvas—if I only had a little time between learning first-year teacher stuff, meeting online certification deadlines, and completing lesson plans, all while getting home (at the very earliest) around 9:00 p.m. Monday through Wednesday. Closer to midnight Thursday and Friday. Not to mention morning workouts on Saturday followed by five or six hours of football film work, and meetings on Saturday and Sunday. A paycheck would have helped me to buy one of those standard, inspirational classroom posters, though. Not like I had time to hang the thing.

The Wicked Administrator of East Texas

Walk-throughs were all the rage at Terrell High School. The superintendent, principals, and other administrators popped in and out as they pleased. About a month into my first year, one of those administrators entered my classroom with a notepad. She was hunched over her clipboard, reading glasses just on the tip of the nose, and scary. We were right in the middle of brainstorming and researching what elements from *High School Musical: The Movie* we could use to generate publicity for our own high school musical based on the movie. (This lesson is detailed later in our journey.)

The Wicked Administrator of East Texas did not get what was happening, called me into the Administration Building to meet with another administrator (our new teacher facilitator) during my one 49-minute conference period. It should be noted that the conference period is sacred: the only time of day to complete any teacher work so as not to have to take it home. The administrator that called this meeting was responsible for new teacher retention, so at least I figured I would not be fired.

"Mr. Mercer," the facilitator began, "one of our administrators was doing a walk-through in your room and had some issues. Students were not engaged as they were watching a movie. There was no student work displayed in the room, and in fact no decorations at all. The only things she noted were the words 'Operation Dumbo Drop' written on the whiteboard, accompanied by random words and phrases

scribbled from top to bottom. Can you imagine what a parent or administrator would think if they walked in your room and saw 'Operation Dumbo Drop' written on the board? What is going on here?"

I responded politely and passionately. I was kind of beat down by this point, trying to stay afloat. It was time to catch my breath. I let the facilitator know that everything in my heart and soul wanted to decorate this classroom. I let her know that I have been working six or seven days a week since July 21, and I did not even have time for a trip to Walmart, let alone any money to spend. The "student work" was the scribble all over the board, and "Operation Dumbo Drop" would be an incredible mass communication project across all of my classes to publicize the first official high school musical in thirty-two years at the Terrell ISD Performing Arts Center—a task requested by the administrator of The Performing Arts Center as he was aware of my radio background and wanted my help marketing the event. "I can get the textbooks out if you prefer," I said, "but this is real world stuff we are doing."

I would also be observed by the online certification company six times that year. Their representative was a retired principal who liked what he saw happening, but did dock me for my room decor, saying that I needed to do a better job of "selling" my content. *Please, just give me a paycheck already.*

If they only knew what I had planned. You see, I was a coach but I loved teaching. There would be nights after a JV game at midnight (once I finally had some money) where I would go buy a doctor's coat for the next day's lesson. Or one morning after another late night of lesson plans and online certification course projects, where I stopped at Walmart before 6:00 a.m. morning workouts to buy balloons and helium tanks. I was a teacher first, and would do whatever it took to do the best job possible.

If only the Wicked Administrator of East Texas, who walked through my room for two minutes before running to tattle on me could see my room now and the numerous "missions," "operations," and "undercover projects" that we have completed!

The classroom is your studio. You have a product to sell, a demographic to reach, and your studio design is every bit as important as your instructional strategy when it comes to engaging, inspiring, and cultivating a classroom environment conducive to exceptional instructional potential.

Touch screen monitors, devices, video streams, couches, multicolor LEDs, demographic-based posters, futuristic desks and decorations, autograph walls and photos from the most memorable experiences: These considerations greeted the casual listener who came to pick up their prize package at the radio station. They entered in awe, and I wanted students to feel the same when entering my classroom. As I designed my classroom, each step of the way I focused on inspiring and innovating with each decorative choice.

I imagined the scene from the original *Willy Wonka*, when Gene Wilder opens the door to the room where everything is edible and the chocolate fountain flows (just before Augustus Gloop spoils the fun). Cross that with all that is inspirational, relevant, and futuristic for a high school demographic, accented by a little bit of Google and PlayStation.

Another of my inspirations for classroom design is the show *Fantasy Factory* on MTV. I have often told my students that when I get rich, I am going to build a Fantasy Factory classroom. It will be the most incredible classroom in the history of the world, complete with zip lines, a fireman's pole, a foam pit, basketball hoops, football targets, putt putt, wifi lounges, and the largest TV screen ever assembled for classroom instruction. The teacher would navigate the room by Segway. I'm not rich yet. We have made some significant classroom enhancements as my students and I have improvised and collaborated to create a new learning environment to better engage our demographic.

My second year teaching, during the first days of school, I shared my idea for a floating tray in which to turn in assignments: anything different, weird, creative, or fun to get students to submit their work. "Maybe even an electric scooter with a basket in front one could drive between the aisles to pick up completed assignments," I said. I wanted students to be engaged with the process of turning in assignments as well. If turning in an assignment was more fun, many more assignments would be turned in, and on time.

A few days later, and under the leadership of senior Elijah Sigler, and at the initiative of Allen Wright, another senior, the

Tray of Wisdom (TOW) was constructed and installed above my desk. I'd walked out of the room for five minutes, and returned to the TOW. Decorated in sacred geometry and fully adjustable and durable, thanks to Allen's engineering. Fishing line suspended the tray from the ceiling, which made turning in assignments not only engaging but more effective. Even better, the students owned the product, process, and solution. It was their way. I now had more room on my desk, the look of the room was enhanced, and ready for the future. Any teachers to this day would benefit from a floating TOW and there was some discussion of students creating a business called Pimp My Inbox.

Next, we needed a place in the room (inspired by the Mix 102.9 Full Throttle Garage) that could be used for coming up with big ideas and creative thinking. I tell my students that you cannot force a genius idea and if you need some time in the Creative Thinking Lounge (CTL) we will make it happen. The CTL is fully equipped with the coolest possible chairs and other furniture available each year. It would evolve accordingly. For example, inflatable furniture is a bad investment. The most effective chair I have found was not my idea at all, but a wonderful Christmas gift from my parents. It is the Gigantic Lawn Chair. Just google Gigantic Lawn Chair and you will be well on your way to securing one of the best classroom furniture pieces possible. Sacred geometry is said to enhance creative thinking, so end tables are covered and posters are strategically placed.

Sacred geometry is an intentional design for stickers, posters, and/or wallpaper that encourages different abilities and qualities depending on the design. I usually choose the design to enhance brain power. In an episode of *Rob & Big* on MTV, Rob Dyrdek, a professional skateboarder, puts these sacred geometry stickers on his skateboard and pulls off some tricks that he had never completed before. My first thought was, *I need some of that magic in my classroom.* Do I really believe in this magical wallpaper? No, not at all. But to this day, students say they feel a much better energy flowing in our classroom.

The first year, the CTL was adorned with a king's throne that by luck I spotted at a resale shop on my way home from work one day. A little gold spray paint, a six-dollar red pillow from Target, and the first official CTL was ready for testing. I can guarantee we had some of the most genius ideas that semester, and students who did not even take my classes often came in and spent time in the CTL to prepare for a test or "charge up" their pencils with the sacred geometry posters.

All of these ideas—an R2D2 that can patrol the room and protect us from outsiders, a hoverboard (updated not to catch fire), and an electric scooter blinged out with a school mascot theme, all have been integrated into our classroom. Professional video, audio, and imaging studios are some of the upgrades utilized over the past few years. The emphasis remains on the look. You can buy an expensive video camera, or you can get a less expensive camera with wrap-around, studio furniture, LED flashing keyboards and mice, and dual screen monitors, and your students will actually look forward to making magic happen.

Portable ping pong, magnetic darts, Nerf basketball goals, guitars, and ukuleles are available. The posters are relatable and student-created. Photoshopped movie posters with our students' faces instead of actors, blueprints of great creative designs like the Batmobile, the Tardis, the Millennium Falcon, and the *Back to the Future* time machine inspire daily, alongside Zelda, Donkey Kong, Mario Brothers stickers, and a Gryffindor flag, waving proudly. The classroom rules are a poster from *Bill & Ted's Excellent Adventure* "Be excellent to each other." Now we have an environment that engages, inspires, and promotes learning at a higher level and we haven't even started instruction!

6 SALES

"You can't put a price on passion. With passion, possibilities are limitless."

I HATED SALES. I wanted nothing to do with it, except for producing commercials. I resisted or evaded the responsibility every time. I wanted to work in the radio station producing on and off the air. I wanted to create content utilizing the music, sound effects, microphones, computers, and other technology. The problem was that to make decent money in smaller markets like Stephenville and Abilene, you had to sell.

Voldemort, my boss at Texas 98, insisted that I give it try, and asked me why I hated it so much. I said that the feeling I would get upon entering a business to sell them something, especially one full of community members that you already know, is terrible. It made me feel disingenuous, and like I am ruining the genuine relationship with the person. I did not like that feeling.

Voldemort said something really great that changed my attitude toward sales, at least enough to sell a few sponsorships for my show and make some extra money.

Voldemort: "Do you like your show?"
Me: "Yes, sir."
Voldemort: "Do you believe that the sponsors of your show benefit from sponsoring your show?"
Me: "Yes, sir."
Voldemort: "Well, it sounds to me like you are helping these people. You are doing them a favor. If they sponsor your show, you will be able to help their business make more money."

Voldemort was right. I quickly realized I could use my creativity to put together various packages, commercials, and strategies to sell sponsoring businesses to the public. I was sold on doing sales. But, only because I believed in my show, and knew that sponsoring the show would translate into more business for the client. If I don't believe in something, I don't sell it.

Teachers likewise have a product to sell, and their "clients" can be just as challenging as the most stubborn business owner.

You Must Love Your Product
- Sell your students on the course, project, or instructional goal.

- Sell your lesson plans.
- Sell every day.
- Do not to take a lot of time—just a few minutes when addressing the class at the start.
- Remind the students of the instructional goal, and challenge the students to go bigger and better than any other student in the history of the course.

To teach like a DJ and sell your product to your students, any part of your instructional design can be the selling point. The course, the lesson plan, and the instructional goal can be experienced in a way to motivate and "sell" your students on your ideas.

Start with your course. From the first day of school, have an "elevator pitch" ready to inspire the students for the adventure in your classroom. Make sure that when the kids go home to tell their parents and guardians about their day, that you and your class steal the show. Take time the first few weeks to sell your course, build the classroom environment, and lay the foundation for incredible buy-in to your course and the journey ahead. All of the extra work you put into selling your course will make a significant impact on student attitudes and results for the entire year.

First-Year Debate Coach

My second year of teaching, I was the new debate coach at Frisco High School. That included teaching Debate I, II, & III, as well as competing in more than ten tournaments during the year across the state. I was very excited for the opportunity. I had no real debate experience. My freshman year of high school, I did take one semester of Debate, but I had to drop out of the course because my teacher insisted that I go to debate tournaments instead of basketball tournaments and I found this unacceptable.

Did I promote this history on the first day of school? No way. I had to sell my team on the notion that we would be the best. I was going to find and emulate the best coaches in the state, and learn everything I could to be the best for my team. We would have the best resources available. We would have an environment conducive to top performance. I would be doing everything possible to give them a chance to be their best. I had some of the most brilliant students you can imagine. It was a real challenge keeping up with this crew.

I had to study, I had to learn how to be successful in all events. Some coaches will only allow students to compete in specific events, but I did not want to place any restrictions on my team. The best way to survive in this scenario and set up the team for success is to challenge your students, hold them accountable, and motivate them to be their best. You can place the responsibility on the student and enable them to prepare, practice, drill, and train as a team. While the team worked, I volunteered at camps and received training from some of the best coaches in the state so that eventually I could bring more to the table for our team.

Selling Multiple Courses

The way your students explore, discover, and learn should be celebrated and practiced. Sell your instructional design by encouraging students to take risks, push the limits, and challenge each other and the instruction as it's happening.

There was a three-year stretch in my teaching career when I was expected to prepare and teach ten different courses, from junior high to high school level. Basically, every single day for three years as a teacher I was teaching multiple courses for the very first time. All instruction was new, innovative, and challenging. I knew little about many of the tools and most of the terminology, and I learned about instruction from the students at the same time they were learning the material, and often they were the ones teaching me.

Together, we consistently produced some of the most innovative instructional experiences. The students went above and beyond my expectations because we did not even know what was really possible, in turn setting a new standard for the next year or semester. The new students were then inspired to go above and beyond their predecessors and we all got better. For each course that was new to all of us (and the ones I might have had a year or two of experience teaching), we always pushed ourselves to use only the newest research and methods. If the real world could do it, we could do it.

By this point, I was not as scared to tell the students that I had no experience teaching a given course, because I had experience providing my students with the opportunity to be the best in the state. I may not have known how to do something, but I knew that if we all worked together, researched together, and shared, we will beat everyone with a textbook and do things that no other school was doing.

Students are way more inspired by and sold on a product that they are the experts and owners of, than any teacher's sales pitch. Now we are teaching students how to be responsible for their own learning. When they have more control of their learning, they will buy in even more so to the course, instructional design, or instructional goal.

SSCP – Super Secret Collabo Project

My second year teaching (and first year at Frisco High School) I went to an after-school workshop hosted by two of the district's Instructional Technology Facilitators. The training was about using new instructional technology tools. I love new technology, and when you can find a teacher training that you are actually interested in, you are already winning.

We left the workshop that day with a homework assignment: to create a lesson plan that utilized a new instructional technology tool. Two weeks later, we would return with our results.

The race was on, and I was about to show everyone how incredible my students were. The other teachers in the room did not know it at the time, but we were in the middle of a serious competition. My students were going to win, and we were going to do some things that had not yet been done, with tools that had not even been used for instructional technology. The most important step would be "selling" my students on the project.

I did not just decide to write a lesson plan that included a new technology tool. We would live the lesson plan and utilize multiple instructional technology tools, ultimately crafting a shared presentation that incorporated an entire unit of instruction and new instructional technology tools (one different tool per student). The instruction would be researched, written, created, produced, and presented by the students. The new knowledge and technology are in action throughout the process and presentation.

In Communication Applications we were starting our Listening Unit. The following class, I gave my sales pitch. "Let's do a project that has never been done before." The students divided the entire unit and new technology tools among themselves designating a collaboration expert who would incorporate all the parts and design the final presentation. They had one week to explore, learn, research, and practice with the content and new technology tool. The second week, they made final touches to their shared creation.

To make the lesson plan more engaging for the students, I made our objective a challenge. We had two weeks. We had to use new instructional technology to complete this project that had never been done before, and we would compete against other teachers. The bonus challenge: The project had to be one hundred percent paperless. I would provide the new technology tools and all instructional resources would be available to research online.

We gave our mission a name "Operation SSCP." I wrote it with UV ink on the whiteboard. (You had to use our hidden UV light pen to read the hidden objective beneath the generic one). It stood for Operation Super Secret Collabo Project, but we only referred to it as SSCP during the two weeks as we wanted to be the first, and could not let our secret out. For one, we couldn't have other teachers stealing our plans, but most importantly, anytime you can make projects "special" (like with a cool name), there is a better chance of an awesome project. A cool name alone will help sell your project by at least ten percent. (I just made up this statistic, but it is true.) Sometimes in radio, a cool name for a bit is the catalyst before even knowing what the bit will be.

Over the next few days, we collaborated and shared our individual final projects with Trent Sandwisch, our student leader. On the final day, the team presented the entire unit through the shared collaboration tool. Each instructional technology tool brought the main ideas of the various lessons included in the Listening Unit to life in real-world situations.

They did it. Given the opportunity to step up and prove themselves, they performed flawlessly. The project was selected as the best in Frisco ISD's Fab Five projects, and presented at the Texas Computer Education Association (TCEA) convention—a project that earned me recognition in Frisco ISD, and led to me being hired as the next Instructional Technology Facilitator for the district.

I wanted to be the best. In the classroom, to be the best, your kids must be performing at their best. For this project, I focused on my sales pitch until it was great and focused the motivation of my students. Remove your expectations, and focus on motivation. The students will always perform well above your preconceived expectations when the limitations of expectations are removed and motivation comes from within.

"The problem with expectations is that there are limitations. Expectations are just higher-level limitations ... If you shoot for the moon, you will miss a lot of other cool things."

You can challenge the students. Shorten the timeline, do the project in a completely new way, or use a tool that is innovative. Design real-life experiments and research projects that recognize the benefits of understanding and creating with new knowledge. Allow students the freedom to explore the content in their own way and relate the information to models and situations that they already enjoy. Students can buy into the instructional goal and sell the project to each other better than you, and when the whole class is sold on the course, project, or instruction, magic will happen.

Challenging the students, and taking time to "sell" the project, product, or instructional goals is more beneficial than the mode of instruction. As the students work away, you can continue to sell their progress. Walk around the room keeping the students motivated with high fives and a positive attitude.

To teach like a DJ, you must believe in your product. If you do not believe in what you are doing, you are going to have a hard time selling anything to your clients, especially if they have no vested interest, or have not already bought into the product. Take time to sell your students on the idea, the journey, the benefits, and the goal, and the students will take care of the rest.

7 MARKETING

"If you know what you are doing, you are not trying hard enough."

EVERY RADIO STATION I worked at the DJs were responsible for the marketing of their show. The website, podcasts, email, Facebook, Twitter, YouTube, and beyond fell to the DJ to keep updated. Our morning show team at Mix 102.9 would work together to come up with ideas to market the show on a large scale. We didn't really have a budget, but we brainstormed many creative ways to increase web traffic, podcast downloads, YouTube hits, and publicity for our show.

The original idea was Mariachi Wake-Up. I would dress as an authentic mariachi musician, show up at the house of the nominated listener with my guitar, and serenade their morning wake-up call. Any listener could email and nominate a loved one that could use a Mariachi Wake-Up on Cinco de Mayo. They would let me into the bedroom of the soundly-sleeping loved one, and I would be the alarm.

I was not a fan of this idea, but thought that if the costume was good enough I might get inspired. Plus, it was the day before Cinco de Mayo so there really wasn't much time to come up with a better idea. After the show, we headed to the costume shop. There it was, right in the middle of the store: a mariachi mannequin fully equipped with scarf and sombrero. They said it was the only one left and asked if I wanted to try it on. I checked for the size of the pants, since I knew the rest would fit well enough. I noticed the pants marked with the number 38 on the inside. My pant size was a 34 at the time, and since this bedazzled costume included a fabulous mariachi belt, I just knew it would work. I was exhausted anyway, and all I wanted was a nap. Waking up at 3:30 in the morning to get to the studio and do all of the show prep was awful, especially on a Friday after a full week.

5:30 a.m., the show prep was completed. It was time to suit up as the Morning Mariachi. Before I could even begin to change, I realized I had forgotten my guitar. I scrambled to call Tony, one of the hosts of the morning show and asked him to bring his Matchbox 20-autographed guitar from his house. Things got worse. I then learned that either the sizing of mariachi pants is on a completely different scale from normal pants, or the number 38 written inside the pants simply denote a random issue number for the costume shop. By no means could I get the pants to fasten. They didn't even come close to meeting in the middle.

Luckily, I had a pair of black workout shorts with me that I put on underneath the pants to disguise the wide-open fly. The guitar could do the rest, so long as I kept the playing contemporary and refrained from rocking out.

Victoria, the other co-host and CW33 Entertainment Reporter at the time, was no help when she arrived. She simply laughed hysterically, almost to tears, and asked me how on earth I would pull this off. When Tony finally showed up, just fifteen minutes before show time, he'd also forgotten to bring the Matchbox 20-autographed guitar.

Down to the wire, Tony and Victoria hatched an even greater plan. It still made use of the ill-fitting costume, and if all went well, would garner us tons of free publicity for the show. The bit would be my "punishment" for not being prepared, and not trying my pants on. They would kick me out of the studio, and I could not return until I'd made it on TV as a mariachi from the Morning Mix. We knew the media would be clamoring for Cinco de Mayo-themed shots.

As I waited for Josh, my driver, to arrive in the Mix 102.9 van, I was greeted by the wonderful Jeff Crilley. At the time, Jeff Crilley was a local news reporter, and author of *Free Publicity*. He handed me a mini portable TV that reporters use on live shots. "One way to pull this off," he suggested, "would be to look for the live shots of the TV stations and crash the scene in your costume." Not a bad idea and this guy is about a nice as they come. Thanks for the help, Jeff Crilley.

Josh showed up and it was go-time. Tony was already ridiculing me on-air and Victoria was still laughing about my misfortunes. But then, some luck! It turned out that Josh-the-driver played guitar as well and he had one in his apartment across the street. I could have kissed him. With a guitar, we might actually have a chance. We picked up his guitar, and my own plan was underway.

During the drama, I remembered that Victory Plaza had recently opened up in downtown Dallas. Channel 7 would be live from 6am to 7am, and their new location had the massive widows like you would see on *Good Morning America*. I instructed Josh to take us to Victory Plaza, sure we would be on TV in no time. Certainly, they would be looking for a mariachi on Cinco de Mayo. I only had to stand outside the window, across from the camera and the hosts, and dance and sing my mariachi heart out.

We made it to the plaza. I ran up the steps like Rocky Balboa to the windows and looked inside like an eager puppy. The director pointed at me, and motioned for me to look at one of the cameras mounted outside the W Hotel across the street. If my plan worked, we would know immediately as there were monitors scattered about and a jumbotron that broadcasts the live show outside the studio. I called Tony to let him know that we were about to make this happen on Channel 7.

Like magic, the anchors were returning from a commercial break. I sang, danced, and strummed like a pro, knowing there would be no audio, only a visual shot. I was broadcasted into homes all over the Dallas area: a glorious Morning Mariachi celebrating Cinco de Mayo live in Victory Plaza for at least ten seconds and maybe more. I had been away from the radio station for fifteen minutes and was already on TV. Time to call back into the show and gloat about how Channel 7 could not resist putting this face on TV.

"Hollywood, just call me Hollywood," I exclaimed as Tony and Victoria took my call live on the air. Before I could say anything else, they shut me down and informed me that I had not been successful. I was supposed to have gotten free publicity for the show. All anyone saw was some hack mariachi acting a fool for ten seconds on live TV.

Everything happened so fast, Josh had forgotten to bring the banner into the shot. As far as the bit went, I was still being punished and could not return until I completed the task, or I would be fired.

I was not in the mood to look for live shots on Jeff Crilley's portable TV. We had to do this big, and the longer I spent away from the station, the longer my work day would be.

"Josh, take us to Fox 4." I said.

Despite ruining our TV appearance, Josh was great. He was a local guy that knew his way all over Dallas. He still works in radio to this day, first taking over my role, and later, the afternoon show at Mix 102.9.

Traffic was picking up; we would not have time to drive anywhere else. I marched into Fox 4's main building. I let the front office know that a producer would want to speak with me. It worked, and I let the producer know that we had a special gift for Megan Henderson and Tim Ryan, *The Good Day Dallas* morning anchors. Not only would I offer my mariachi services for Cinco de Mayo, I but I had written a beautiful song to celebrate their 5 years together on the show. I told Josh to be ready. "Forget the banner, that might scare them off. But stay by my side." He had a mix 102.9 shirt on that would be less invasive. "These TV people can be a little finicky."

The producer informed me that she knew who I was, and exactly what was going on. She had been listening all morning and felt sorry for me. She would return and let me know if I would be able to sing my five-year anniversary Cinco De Mayo mariachi song. Great news. *Now I need to write a song.* I did not have a song. Originally, I was only going to be waking people up with this bit, I didn't need a song, but I had to tell the producer *something* to guarantee I could get on TV.

The producer returned about five minutes later. I was so stressed that there was no way I could have written and memorized a song—but she didn't need to know that. She informed me that they had a real mariachi band performing in the next hour and did not want me to appear as if I am making fun of mariachis. But, they could present me as the gift, and as an attempt to perform for Megan and Tim while the security guard (that already had his eyes locked on me) would be blocking my entrance. The hosts would see the live feed of me trying to get in as a singing, dancing mariachi from Mix 102.9.

The next minute and a half was broadcast on the number-one TV morning show in the Dallas / Fort Worth Metroplex. Not only was Mix 102.9, Tony's, Victoria's, and my name were mentioned several times, but Josh snuck in a shot with his Mix T-shirt for good measure.

The lessons I learned on this day did not come from any textbook or communications course. The real lesson lay not in remembering my guitar, or always to try on my mariachi pants, but in teaching like a DJ. That is, running with the new and better ideas and taking advantage of free publicity through mass media.

Operation Dumbo Drop

During my first year teaching at Terrell High School, I was approached by the administrator of the Terrell ISD Performing Arts Center. He had heard about my radio background and hoped that as a Communication Applications teacher I would be able to help promote the first high school musical to be performed by Terrell High School in more than thirty years. He suggested that we design and distribute posters to help get the word out, as he wanted this to be a wonderful and successful event.

Well, he was right. And, he came to the right place. However, posters were not exciting to me. If my students were going to be involved, we were going to do it big. Every year an opportunity seems to present itself to make magic happen in the classroom. I am always looking for this chance, and when it comes along we go all in, and they always make it happen!

We jumped right into our Mass Communication unit. We researched our product, determined our demographic, and promoted the musical like it was our own Superbowl. I reached out once again to the great Jeff Crilley and his book *Free Publicity* and my students learned all mass communication. We really had no other choice. There was no budget for marketing.

Given the popularity of the *High School Musical* movies at the time, and the fact that our musical would indeed be *High School Musical*, I had to sell this project well. It would be massive, extensive, and challenging. But, if I did my part effectively on the front end, I would learn for the first time in my career that the kids will make it happen above and beyond your expectations every time.

Let the research, brainstorming, and mass communication project begin. We investigated every way possible to communicate our message. We analyzed our demographic, and researched themes, colors, graphics, fonts, every single essential element for effective verbal and nonverbal communication strategies.

It only took a few days for our free publicity plan to come together. My genius students collaborated on the idea of a massive balloon launch carrying a prize-pack including a pair of tickets to *High School Musical*. Sponsors were contacted, radio, TV, and newspapers outlets were notified of the launch date and times. Websites, blogs, and emails were designed and composed using effective communication strategies. Research taught us that it would take 97 standard balloons filled with helium to lift a one-pound load of cargo into the skies.

To help motivate and inspire my students, the least I could do was to allow them to name this project. It was so epic only an incredible code name could do it justice. "Operation Dumbo Drop" remains one of my favorite projects to this day.

This was about the time that the aforementioned Wicked Administrator of East Texas would walk through. She might not have liked the process, but the results could not have been any better. The day of the launch was one of the most rewarding experiences for me as a teacher. My students made the front page of the *Terrell Tribune*, in a story about the *High School Musical* performance and balloon launch. In actuality, it was probably too windy that day as the balloons raced from the center of the 50-yard line of the practice field, barely cleared a potentially disastrous crash into the bleachers, but magically rocketed straight up at the last minute. Tears, cheers, and celebrations commenced. The media was there to capture the anticipation, excitement, and jubilation of the students' successful launch.

The following day, Mr. Dumas (my Assistant Principal) conducted his walk-through of my class, having not yet heard the news. I was passing out newspapers to all of the students in my class as we recapped our lesson and celebrated the utilization of effective mass communication. Ultimately, we sold out all three shows of *High School Musical*. Mr. Dumas was speechless. Take that, Wicked Administrator of East Texas.

Everyone on campus, in the district, and community should know what it means to take your course. All should be aware of the benefits and experiences possible when a child is enrolled in your course. Have an online presence. Be present in the school and exemplify your course's principles. It should be the case that when you are meeting parents, students, and community members outside of your classes, they say, "Oh that's the class where …" Blog to showcase student work. Share your students' projects and successes with local news media. Implement community-based learning and projects.

I have a website for parents and community members to see what occurs in our classroom. Share and collaborate with community members online and provide opportunities for businesses and students to collaborate throughout instruction. The community should know what incredible things are going on in your classroom.

The word of mouth alone from enthusiastic students will be the most powerful tool. Student success should be the Taj Mahal of your classroom. Wall space, websites, and Google Classroom should be covered with incredible student work. Make a "Wall of Glory" with full-color, digital artifacts created by your students that document and recount successful, missions, quests, and adventures. Your classroom and beyond is the product you are marketing: student successes, accomplishments, team and group activities.

Marketing yourself will be easier than you can imagine at this point. When you market your course and your students throughout the school and community, by default, you look good. The work of the students is the goal, and when they shine, you shine just as brightly. Believe in the students, show off the students, and the marketing of your program will be the result.

8 PROMOTIONS
(GAMES, PRIZES, & SWAG)

"If you mess up going 100% in my classroom, you'll get 100% for your grade."

"You're listening to KTCH 101.1, the station that engages students all day every day. Speaking of today, how about this hour? You can win meet-and-greet passes and tickets to see Taylor Swift live at the American Airlines Center. Right now, it's Robin Thicke, 'Blurred Lines,' on KTCH The Teach 101.1."

IT WAS FASCINATING, the range of events and promotional prizes available to listeners in Dallas, versus those in the Abilene and Stephenville markets. On Mix 102.9 I gave away vacations and prize packages valued at several thousand dollars. At KCUB 98.3 FM, we once had a promotion to give away 98.3 cent gas to listeners that had a KCUB bumper sticker. Gas was close to three dollars a gallon back then and we had lines at the pumps. From hosting live events at the Stephenville Town & Country Bank, I upgraded to reserving the Dallas Stars team jet and a Southwest Airlines terminal to construct the North Pole to provide Christmas wishes for underprivileged families. Creating the giveaways and promotions for Larry Joe Taylor Festival tickets at KCUB radio to giving away Christian Louboutin shoes and Saint Laurent handbags at Mix 102.9 may seem very different, but the goal is always the same.

On and off the air you want to create events and experiences for the listeners. Celebrations for all to enjoy. Some of the events may be at a local venue. Some may be at or near the radio station. Many may be promoted and experienced during the show, on the air. The promotions all have one thing in common: the opportunity for the listening audience to be a part of the show or event. One way or another the audience has the chance to celebrate, participate, or win as the station, show, or event is promoted. To teach like a DJ, create great promotions for your students to make more classroom experiences.

One radio game that was once a great success we called the "World's Loudest Dryer Competition." Listeners would call in, place whatever they thought would make the most noise in their dryer and run it with the phone capturing the crashes. After I realized that some were using their dryers at work, I retired the game. Turns out, it's hard to beat thousands of money jar pennies. Dumbbells and ball bearings are great competition, but the pennies were incredibly noisy. The dumbbells did destroy a dryer in a local fitness center.

My favorite game to play on the air was "What Would You Do?" It was easy to run from the DJ's perspective. Basically, if you had some backstage passes to the Larry Joe Taylor Music Festival, and even better, three pairs of tickets, you had guaranteed show material for at least two days. The DJ would open up the phone lines like a teacher with an open-ended, quality question and ask the listeners to call in with their own ideas of what they would do to win the tickets. I usually allowed twenty minutes for the listeners to call in with their proposals, then teased the audience with clips of phone calls between songs, and during commercial breaks. After the call window had closed, I'd pick the top candidates, and allow all of them to complete their "What Would You Do" ideas the next day during the Game of the Day, live on the air.

Prizes were the lifeblood of a radio show and a way to integrate the listening audience into the show on a daily basis. A show could go bigger and better with some sweet prizes. If the news, pop culture, and weather were running slow, then it just took a good "Worlds Loudest Dryer Competition" to bring up the ratings. If I had some really good tickets, we would play "What Would You Do?" One day we had three sets of tickets gearing up for the big weekend push and we shaved the station call letters into one guy's head. Someone hula-hooped in the street for the entire show, and another group had a picnic in the parking lot and ate a hotdog with *whatever* ingredients I could find in the radio station.

I always loved something visual, as we were near a main road and we could drum up some curious new listeners. We had parking lot dance competitions, celebrity look-alike contests, jousting for tickets, and Jello swimming pools to name a few. Of course, you would need to add some great audio potential. Listeners called in promising to pour buckets of water over their bosses' heads. Or, throw the office microwave off of the building. To keep the game of the day topical and relatable to our demographic as a classic rock station, listeners sometimes found themselves speaking with Elvis as they played "Elvis Trivia" against other listeners.

Another on-air promotion I liked at KCUB was the chance to become a member of the Afternoon Saloon Crew. The name for my four to seven shift at Texas 98 was chosen via an on-air promotion and competition. The winner selected Afternoon Saloon and became the very first member inducted into the Afternoon Saloon Crew (ASC). We added one new member every Friday who went above and beyond with any aspect of the show. Calling in, requests, participation, winning—whatever they were the best at, they had a chance to be an even bigger part of the show. Every Friday we would name the ASC members and the newest member would be awarded a special prize package, an ASC mug, and would take the ASC oath. If there was ever any drama or world problems that needed to be solved, we could always reach out to the ASC and get the matter resolved. The main point of this promotion for me was creating a sense of community, a team, and a group that would work together to promote and enjoy the show every day. If the listening audience felt that they were a part of the process, had a say, and believed in the show, then the audience would only grow as more and more listeners were recruited.

Promotions in the classroom are every bit as helpful and have a great potential to make sure your students are part of the team and celebrated. None of these specific games would work well in a classroom, but you can still use competition, prizes, rewards, and incentives to promote learning and make a difference. By turning the final project into an event worth fabulous prizes, suddenly the cool kid who never wants to join in will be motivated by their competitive nature or the chance to earn bonus points. At least now the student can say, "Oh I will do that for five bonus points." They probably wanted to participate the whole time. This occurs often.

Sometimes, I raise the bonus points for a new, uncharted game, or offer triple point Thursdays. First-time presenters double-point day was popular. On that particular day, I reached another personal goal. We had so many new bonus games under our belt and about twenty minutes that we could use for fun; AKA, I'd created an optimal classroom environment.

I use the Game of the Day in the classroom. It may not even relate to the content, but often does. I just make sure that the prizes or game itself will be engaging to our student demographic. When the students are working hard, and doing the right thing, a reward is necessary. Take a moment and provide a brain break. Watch for the point where students become restless—it's time for the Game of the Day. Get the blood flow going, by playing trashketball (basketball with the trash can). Or do a quick review assessment trivia game and make it rain bonus points! As a Communication Applications teacher, we would play games, much like those in *Whose Line Is It Anyway* and relate the communication strategy to the daily objective.

Another Walkthrough

Terrell was big on this walk-through phenomenon. As an emergency-certified first year teacher and new to the district, I also had eight formal observations. Principals, superintendents, and district people were constantly in and out of my class. I love it now. I am always looking for ways to show off what our kids are doing. My first year, I am just hoping I'm not doing something wrong and end up fired. In radio, you had friends, parents, relatives, coaches, bosses, managers, and owners listening all the time. A walk-through would consist of a phone call and a "Hey, great job, that was funny." Or, "Hey, don't play that song."

I guess word got out about something in my class. I was too naive to know what or why. Anytime I have ever been called to the office, I have never known if it would be good or bad. I thought that everything I was doing was right. I was doing my best. I learned a long time ago when I would be nervous before a football game, that all I had to do was my best and I would not have to worry about anything. That is how I teach.

Mr. Washington, an Assistant Principal at Terrell High School, approached me during one class and said that he wanted to see these activities that I do at the end of class. I said, "No problem, just come back near the end and we will do our thing." In the back of my mind, I was like, *No way. What is going on here? This is what I had envisioned my class to be like. Don't take this away from me. What could be wrong?* I mean, I know it may not be in the lesson plan or district curriculum, but this is what sold me on the class in seventh grade. I did make sure to relate each new game to the instructional goal—worst case, that should justify the activity.

Mr. Washington showed up. All 6'6" of him. He was massive and could look into your room without entering as he was tall enough to peek through the windows above the lockers. The students were brilliant, collaborating, creating, analyzing, evaluating, all of the things that I learned later were a good thing. It was the first time that what had seemed right, logical, and appropriate to me was right on. He was cracking up, and I gave all of my students five bonus points for being awesome. It turns out that this is exactly what the district wanted to see. This was an example of how they wanted classroom instruction to be. I thought I was going to get in trouble, but they were actually telling each other, "You need to go and see what is going on in this classroom."

I started with bonus points. It was so easy to just sporadically pass them out for anything. Good attitude, correct answer, collaboration, correcting the teacher, trying out the latest new dance move, or wearing a Tarleton State University shirt. Bonus points proved to be a way for kids who were typically not motivated.

Brain breaks are another way to integrate games and prizes into instruction. I prefer to keep the majority of the breaks related to the instructional goal, but not always. If I can take time to share, relate, or motivate the class to get involved in anything, and to improve the classroom environment, it will be just as beneficial to improve learning as any instructional strategy. We'll play portable ping pong, basketball, magnetic darts, as we move around brainstorming, creating, and innovating. We practice the creative process. Take time to be motivated by the best idea. Then, the work, the learning, and the experiences will occur naturally and with passion.

I remember as a student, high school discussions were mostly teacher-led, formal, tedious, boring, almost painful. I knew the answers. I usually read the passages at my desk when asked only because it seemed to be the only way to survive the boredom. The only time I was motivated at all to join the "not" fun was when the teacher was being observed. In those circumstances, I had someone to impress and a reason to answer the prompts. I was about to show the principal that I was a winner, and I did. That night, at family dinner, I knew good and well what I had done. I was telling my family that, "Yeah, I had a big day. Pretty much blew my teacher's, principal's, and classmate's minds with an answer. No big deal."

What was funny was that being from a small town, my superpowers had already reached my mother. She was shopping at HEB after work, ran into my teacher (I didn't even know they knew each other) and my teacher said, "I just want you to know that during my observation today, your son showed a flash of brilliance." The teacher would have seen many more flashes if she had created a better classroom environment that wasn't so sterile.

Bonus games actually started before bonus points. I had a seventh-grade speech teacher and one of those magical classes with my best friends and students who loved to put on a show. We did specific presentation games, and exercises, like impromptu, pantomime, and speeches in front of the class. We loved it and looked forward to any chance to be allowed to play the games. I knew in seventh grade that if I was ever a Speech teacher I would certainly include this part in my instruction.

Basically, this was my main act starting my first year at Terrell High School. I would introduce the lesson, we would do some related activity, and if all went well, it was BONUS time. We would play multiple bonus games.

I would even play games when I saw my students in the hall during passing periods. Turns out, games became the goal, motivation, and reason for getting work completed. My goal was to create a classroom environment where all students would be unafraid to give their formal speeches, as that would be my final exam. By the end of the first year, we had a chart with more than twenty bonus games.

Inflation for bonus points held steady at two per game for your first one, and one point for each additional game. I offered double point specials for students who had not yet participated. New games, or more challenging games, also went for double points. I can remember one specific time that a student who had never participated stood up and said, "I'm gonna get my points right now. I need to use them on the test." I'd been warned by other teachers that this student would not ever want to speak in front of the class.

Jousting for Tickets and Beat the DJ (teacher) are games adapted from the radio promotions that have been played in my classroom. Make the games real and fun. Create promotions in the classroom. Celebrate milestones, plan parties for days of student presentations. Popcorn makes all instruction better, and it's not terribly expensive. Big events take place all the time at school for extracurricular activities, and award ceremonies. Create events in the classroom promoting all of the wonderful accomplishments and successful quests completed throughout the instructional journey. Work hard and push the students, but take the time to celebrate the wins and victories!

9 ENGINEERING

"It's like when they landed on the moon, they didn't know how to do it, they just did it."

I KNOW THE TRUE MEANING of cut and paste: splicing reel to reel recordings for Dairy Queen commercials, post-game replays, and audio editing where you would actually cut the tape, remove the unwanted audio, and tape it together. Sound effects, station identification, and commercials played with cart machines. If you do not know, cart machines are like eight tracks. If you don't know what eight tracks are, do not worry but just appreciate it when you can skip to a song immediately when you want it played.

Almost every summer, in the middle of the heat, and typically during the July 4th holidays, the radio station would be knocked off the air. The transmitter would overheat due to a dying air conditioner. The shed that the transmitter was housed in was way out in the country with a small air conditioner running non-stop all summer to ensure the transmitter would stay cool. I, out of necessity, learned how to restart and adjust the transmitter, and how to replace air conditioning units, all while dodging wasps.

KCUB very slowly and very gradually upgraded their radio equipment and computers. At one point, I was asked to build an entirely new radio station on the floor above KCUB, a true challenge. Building a radio station proved to me that to do something big, you do not need to know how to do it, you just had to make it happen. This same barrier presents in the classroom, when in the first couple of weeks, as students are not comfortable without step-by-step instructions. If you teach yourself the process and the steps, you will truly learn and at a much higher level. By the way, Real Country 89.7 FM is actually still up and running to this day. You're welcome, Stephenville and surrounding areas.

My first year at Mix 102.9, I was asked to cover the Dallas Mavericks media day that would be held before their practice. An engineer handed me a new digital portable recorder. Upon arrival, I interviewed Jason "The Jett" Terry, Coach Avery, Josh Howard, and Dirk Norwitzski. Before leaving, I listened to the playback and realized that I had not recorded Dirk's interview. Honestly, that was the only interview we wanted, and the only interview we were really going to use on the air. So, I worked my way back to the start of their practice, stopped Dirk on the court just after a warm-up layup, and asked to interview him, again, as I did not actually record his interview. In his thick German accent, with a slightly disappointed look but caring heart he stated, "You are kidding me. (Pause) Okay." Dirk redid the interview for me underneath the basketball goal and became my favorite basketball player of all time.

The following year, I would be asked by The FOX Network to travel to Los Angeles for three days to interview more than fifty of the stars of their upcoming fall lineup. An engineer would once again send me off with an even more sophisticated portable recording and live broadcasting studio. I would still be live in the mornings on Texas time, 4:00 a.m. California, and record about twenty interviews each day. In all the chaos of broadcasts, interviews, hanging out with John Rzeznik, the lead singer of the Goo Goo Dolls, I only messed up about half of the interviews. Fred Willard insisted on using a different microphone, so I was able to get his, but forgot to switch the controller back to the correct microphone for most of day two.

As the technology improved throughout my radio career, I grew more and more appreciative of having the engineers around. Every time when I would be out and about making appearances or interviewing someone for the radio station, the engineers would have everything set up and ready to go. All of the live bands and performances for concerts and on-air performances would go off without a hitch. These engineers knew their stuff.

So, as a teacher passionate about new technology integration, I used the engineer strategy myself. I was not going to be the one responsible for making it all work effectively. My engineers would be trained, willing, and able to ensure we were using the latest and greatest technology we could get our hands on to enhance learning and engage.

Another Trip To The Office

The second time I got called to the AP's office was due to my incredible classroom engineers. The special part about this day was that a student, Ashley Thompson, volunteered to run everything. I could just observe and keep track of the bonus points. She knew the rules, and how to introduce games, switch games, provide all students opportunities and keep everything positive. Ashley had a microphone, as if she was hosting a game show. Some of the games required a microphone and we liked to make it like a game show anyway. Plus, I wanted the kids to get familiar and lose the fear of speaking into a microphone in a natural, fun way.

That's when I received another email from Mr. Antwine that I needed to meet him, in his office. I went first chance. *Here we go again,* I thought. I just never knew. Would I be praised or fired? Again, I had not spent any time in other teachers' classrooms. Nor did I want to. I liked doing things my way. My way, made sense. I was experimenting and we were doing big things.

Mr. Antwine had received a complaint from the classroom next door. We were just too loud. He wanted to know why on earth I was using a microphone. If classroom management was such a problem that a microphone was necessary, we had other issues to address. He also let me know that the room next door was a reading class. Students sat in silence and read and when microphones, music, videos, and clapping happened, it was very disrupting.

I apologized, said I would not use the microphones, and went back to my room with my tail between my legs. If my boss asked me to do something, I asked no questions and did what I was told. But, this time I did know that in a communication class, using microphones was a benefit. Also, manipulating electronics for sound effects, music, and other tools was important to formal presentations. I mean, how many times have you gone to a presentation and the first ten minutes is the awkward presentation transition period, trying to get the video, projector, or microphone to work? My students were using our state of the art DJ studio/presentation station to facilitate their activities. I turned around to track down my Mr. Antwine again. I didn't care if they sent my class out to the shed, or the Ag barn. I believed in what we were doing.

Nothing could be done that year. But the next year they moved the other teacher away, and we were back in business. To this day, I average about one noise complaint per year (Sorry, Mr. Adams). I do not like quiet classrooms.

When the students are the engineers, they are enabled to explore and discover, utilizing new instructional tools, technology, and equipment. The students are forced to learn and teach. Also, student engineers help to make the class run more smoothly. Need a class DJ or a student to lead an activity? They will be ready to go. If you do not have time to explore new technology, new instructional tools, or even manage parts of your daily classroom activities, the engineers will get things done for you.

One of the best reasons to use student engineers is that by the time they test and report back about the new tools, you will be able to learn the new tools more quickly as they can simply show you the basic functionality. We even set up for the ability to broadcast our lessons live, or provide pre-recorded daily content for homebound students who wanted to be part of the classroom instruction. Keeping in mind, most often when I say "we," I mean the students capture, edit, share, or do what is necessary to make these things happen. All technical problems, issues, and challenges can be passed to your team of engineers. Bonus points are free, and everyone learns and gets better. Never again will I have to stop Dirk mid-layup, as I will have a team of engineers ready to make it happen right the first time.

The students who finished early, the students who wanted extra credit, and the students who had a desire to learn more about technology or who had a special knack for it had every possible opportunity to be the engineers. I thought of them as a team of researchers in the labs, testing new instructional technology tools, exposing the limitations and challenges of browsers, logins, email verifications, software, apps, devices, and blocked websites or programs. Students made the presentation—for the next presentation—using the new presentation tool. The lesson provided an example of the new tool that the students would be utilizing. The students became the experts and made themselves available to the entire class as the new technology tool was adopted.

Likewise, student aids in my classes got their hands on the latest and greatest. They were challenged to innovate and revamp all of my instructional resources. My second year at Frisco High School, I was still using original PowerPoints given to me at Terrell High School. No more. Aids helped to integrate all of my instructional material, audio, video, examples, and files into one complete web-based presentation tool. PowerPoints and paper were shunned and known as "bad words," never be used again in our classes. We eradicated all evidence of PowerPoints by spring of 2010. And, after testing the waters that spring, and again during two summer school sessions, the decree was issued that paper would never again be used for instruction.

It didn't make any more work for me and actually improved my life. I believe paperless is the only way to go. Not only for teachers, but for our students. Students need to be preparing for the technology of the future and how business will be conducted in the future. Students gain more by utilizing the instructional technology available in the labs, or on the devices in their pockets, than from books, paper, or PowerPoints.

My first year at Dripping Springs, Texas, they offered me four courses that were new to me. In addition to updating their Broadcasting program, I would be teaching Animation I, Print & Imaging Technology, Principles of Audio & Video Technology, and Advanced Audio & Video Production. I would have a budget to manage, our own server and network to maintain and manage, video cameras, chargers, microphones, headphones, teleprompters, tripods, camera bags, and fifteen years of old equipment, books, paper, and junk to sort. The computer lab had twenty-four iMacs (and for those of you that have not made the PC-to-Mac switch, it is not exactly seamless when you are the brand new fancy technology teacher on campus). Upon, the end of my first semester, I suddenly realized that, except for Debate, I had never even taught a year-long course before. I would just have to keep designing instruction and pushing these kids. I was nervous and worried that teaching so many new courses would wear me out.

Karen Tiller, the school librarian, had an empty room available in the back of the library. She knew of my radio background and asked if I could build a radio station for them. I said no problem. I had always wanted to build one at any of my schools, but was just too busy with instructional design. I was already drowning in Dripping Springs … but I remembered what I had learned about the abilities of a good set of student engineers. Within the school year, Tiger Radio, KROR "The Roar" was on the air. The kids did it. They built the radio station. I knew how, but they did it, and now they know how.

At this point, seven years into teaching, I'd worked in four different districts, as a teacher, coach, and an administrator at the junior high and high school levels and had taught at least fourteen different courses. The 2015-2016 school year would be the most challenging year for me as a classroom teacher. To pull it off with my sanity intact, I would need a classroom full of engineers.

First period was Broadcast Journalism, the official name for the "Radio" class, as everything we needed to build the station had been ordered and was ready to be built. First period would also be another round of Print & Imaging, and a handful of Advanced Audio & Video Production, the gradebook name for our "Tiger Daily News" broadcast class that all others would take during second period.

I survived teaching three courses during first period, including building the radio station, by insisting that our radio class be the engineers tasked with building the radio station on their own as I had done when I was twenty-four. They made it happen.

During second period, our *Tiger Daily News* (TDN) class for Advanced Audio & Video Production scripted, recorded, edited, and produced the daily announcements during the forty-nine minute class period. TDN was also tasked with producing videos to supplement the daily announcements covering school, events, athletics, organizations, and developing even more advanced productions. Teachers, administrators, and community members constantly reached out to have our students film and edit various projects. Just as any broadcasting company would do, I passed along the information to our engineers and they would make it happen, all while producing the daily news announcement video on time and effectively.

Third period was even more challenging for me, as Animation

I and Animation II were stacked. I am still terrible at Animation. If the students had any clue about my real animation abilities, there is no way they would be as incredible as they are in these courses. Somehow, I pulled it off that first year in Animation I. I had a full year of lessons and incredible artifacts to prove it, but the party was not over. Year two began with even more sophisticated and elaborate animation to learn. Fortunately, I already had some of my best engineers ever in my Animation II class. Turns out, it was a better instructional strategy to allow them to facilitate the instruction for much of the Animation I class. Incredible projects were designed that year.

Fourth period's Principles of Audio & Video Technology went over well. A full class, I had to place one student enrolled in Advanced Animation in the production studio so each student could have a computer. (By the way, the Advanced Animation student had not even taken regular Animation)

I wish I could have stopped there, but fifth period was Cinematography, a course that gave Advanced Audio & Video or Principles of Audio & Video students an opportunity to train even more for movie, film, and cinema technology. It meant another new course for me to design, and a challenging one, as Journalism was a qualified prerequisite at the time, so half of my students did not even know how to operate a camera or edit video. But even that's not a problem, when you can rely on your student engineers to be responsible for training all students on how to use our equipment.

Sixth period earned the title of "Chosen Class" that year. They were machines, like all of my students, but this group was a great team. Maybe it was because I had the most experience teaching Principles of Audio & Video, or because it was the only course in my day that I taught more than once, and sixth period was the second time, so I had a pretty good idea what we would be doing instructionally. Every one of those courses, by the way, use different software, devices, technology, chargers, adapters, microphones, headphones, batteries, websites, and instructions—meaning we had to clean it all up for Cinematography, drag it all out again for sixth period, then clean it up again for first period the next day. Again, not a problem, as your student engineers can make it happen for you.

Designing instruction that was innovative and challenging for all these courses that I had never taught fell to the students in the class. On the front end, we would come up with the greatest animation goals possible. I then set the students free to attack the instructional goals their way. These students were enabled and challenged to find a way to create and learn far above and beyond the step-by-step instructions in the book.

To protect my sanity, health, and quality of life, I had no choice but to give the students more control over their learning. Turns out, that is the best way to teach ... Collectively, the students will always know more than I do. Each year, their projects are more spectacular and better than any I could have imagined (and I am a creative person). The student engineer can make dreams a reality in the classroom. Learning can come to life when students are enabled.

Year one, I taught from a single laptop. Year two, a five computer PC lab. Then a full PC lab. In year four, we had access to a class set of iTouches. Then a PC lab at the junior high, followed by a Mac lab at the high school. Not only was my instruction changed, updated, and improved every year, but the tools were adopted to enhance learning at the highest level possible. My student engineers trained me and updated all of our instructional resources and tools. My student engineers make me look good all the time now.

The secret is putting the responsibility on the students and allowing them to be the experts.
- Photography and video cameras of multiple designs and functionality.
- Teleprompters, boom mics, lenses, and tripods.
- Exporting and importing.
- SD cards, flash drives, usb cables, adapters, and converters.
- Compress, unzip, crop, save, share.
- Mpeg, mp4, m4a, mp3, mov.
- Update website, turn it into the server, upload it to the cloud, save it on Google Drive, email, DropBox, Google Classroom, wrong link.

It is the responsibility of the engineers.

Now that I have taught for nine years, and have almost as much teaching experience as radio experience, everything is done by my students. If we build a recording studio and radio station at the school, they did it. If we are the first Debate team to convert all of our files to digital and only carry laptops to competitive events, it is because students make it happen. When we want to get a 3D printer for our inventions and create a scale 3D model of the school, my student engineers are the ones to teach me how we can make it happen and they make it happen.

The powers of the student aide are often underutilized. A student aide can start a classroom hype squad. This can be a club that is tasked with the purpose of generating excitement in the classroom. A student aide can help you take your classroom into the future with new technology, decor, and instructional tools guaranteed to engage at a higher level. Not having money or a budget is less a problem, if you get a club and student aides running in the same direction. Turn these student aides, students eager for bonus, or students who finish early, into classroom engineers accomplishing real-world and difference-making projects.

10 SHOWTIME!

"Smile, you are teaching!"

A FEW LIGHTS DANCE across the control board. Soon, the automated broadcast will fade out and transition to the live, local show. One of two large, touch-screen monitors begins to flash counting down the last ten seconds before the show starts. The new show introduction is cued up to play. You have prepped the last hour to make sure your show content is packed and produced for your listening audience. You fire off the show intro on the air, turning your mic on but keep it faded down until you are ready to go live. You have about two minutes of content to fill, not a gap of dead air. The transition is smooth, seamless, and on-point. The show has officially started and you are live in 3, 2, 1...

It's easy to go live on the air if you ever make your way into a radio station. Find microphone one, turn it on, and turn it up. The real challenge is getting the show kicked off the right way, getting your listening audience hyped and setting the tone for the rest of the show. The show intro is where you set the tone. It's your chance to sell your audience on not missing a minute of the day's show.

"You are listening to Teach Like a DJ on KTCH 101.1. I'm BJ the DJ along with my trusty sidekick, Dunce Boy. Say hello, Dunce Boy. 'Hello, Dunce Boy.' It's just after 3:00, and we will be with you all the way home with some of the greatest news and information to keep you excited and informed about the most fun and innovative ways to teach like a DJ. The phone lines are open, call us now at 866-436-KTCH. Maybe you're more of the texting type. Get it, texting type. Text us anytime, and we will receive your message in real time, here in the studio. We will surprise one of you today as one of you will be named today's Teacher Of The Show. We are just ten minutes away from the Game of the Day and your chance to win a ten-thousand-dollar classroom makeover. Stacy Labowski will be stopping by in the five o'clock hour to explain how she got every student in her entire gradebook to earn a one hundred for the semester by painting her car school colors. Your requests, as always, in the six o'clock hour, as you will DJ the show one song at a time. It's your

project-based instruction and your chance to teach me, because we all know that teaching others demonstrates a high level of understanding. Right now, it's Bruno Mars, 'Happy' on KTCH 101.1, engaging students all day, every day."

The clock is always the focal point from the control board. Knowing the time is very important on the air. I remember a clever sign next to the clock at my first radio station with the message, "Smile, you are on the radio," and an emoji smiley face next to it. My first thought was *This has got to be a joke*. Like a meme that was ahead of its time. Pretty funny that the most prominent sign in the studio instructed the DJ to do the one thing that none of my audience could even see. Eventually, someone explained to me the theory behind the sign. If you are smiling as you are talking on the air, it will sound like you are happy and in a good mood to your listeners. It will actually make you sound more upbeat on the air.

Smile, You Are Teaching!
The same goes in the classroom, and more so, because the students actually see you. If you are smiling, your students will feed off of your energy. During your class intro, you can set the tone for the day. Let the students know what they will love about this class. Sell them on the instruction and make them believe that they will benefit by being a part of the instruction. Providing a solid intro to get your students excited about the instruction will make a huge difference in buy-in and classroom productivity. They need to

believe, and when you teach like a DJ, your intro is a difference-maker.

The Show Intro and the Daily Objective

Play some music to get the class started. Talk over an instrumental music bed. Get your class DJ to drop some sick beats and introduce the teacher on the mic. And, when you do "turn on the mic" (i.e. begin to talk), be at your best. I mean it. You need to bring it, and let everyone know that it will be the best class period ever.

Welcome everyone. Share a real-life story that your audience can relate to and appreciate, like, "You will never believe what happened to me last night," or "Guess what happened on the way to work." Make sure your audience knows what is coming, what they must be a part of and would hate to miss. Kick the show off with a game, or bit to immediately grab your audience's attention. Get them excited, fired up, and impatient for the next time you open the mic.

First Break

To teach like a DJ, your intro and first break should occur before and during the presentation of the day's warm-up activity, agenda, instructional goals, objective, and tasks. The intro is the most important part of the instruction. It sets the tone for the day and an entire project. If the teacher is not excited about it, the students won't be either. What are we doing? Why are we doing it? And, how much fun are we going to have? Get creative, do it big, and the students will take care of the rest.

"Lesson plans are made to be broken."

You need a plan, a strategy for engaging your students and keeping them "tuned-in" for the entire class period. The best lesson plans are fluid, evolving, and enhanced on-the-fly every class period of every day. Teaching is a practice, and the best teachers adapt their instructional design and strategy continuously. If you are bored with the lesson plan for the day, the students will be bored. Change it. Even on my way to work I've thought, *I'm not excited about the day's lesson or activity. I'm going to change it*. Once I was excited again, and could not wait to enter the classroom, I knew we were back on the right track.

Never give "busy-work." Give them a real problem to solve. They will be motivated to solve the problem even if it's significantly more challenging. When they know you are not going to waste their time, they will not waste yours. Busy-work causes discipline problems and bad teaching.

Just as the show intro is utilized to set the tone and excite the listeners for what is on the way, the first break maintains the momentum and keeps the audience on their toes. The first break should be just as purposeful, specific, interactive, and relatable as the show itself.

When you "break" in radio you address your audience with a purpose. The average music DJ takes five breaks per hour. A morning show music DJs may have breaks averaging three minutes or more. Afternoon DJs typically take shorter breaks. You do not break just to talk. You have an intention.

Every time you open the mic you need to be "on." Speak with purpose. I once tried to correct Adam Levine, a judge on *The Voice*, and lead singer for Maroon 5, after he made a mistake recording liners. When he told me, "Yes, I know. I've done this before," I felt pretty ridiculous, as he has easily spent more time recording in studios than I have, and probably records radio station liners daily. I was wasting his time and this led to him getting frustrated with me and the process. Adam made the mistake, but I was the one who looked like an idiot.

When you speak to your students it counts; they want to listen. When you speak it is engaging, meaningful, and not "dead air." Do not waste their time. Respect their time and yours. Remove all unnecessary, repetitive communication. Always have something purposeful or engaging to share when delivering procedures, expectations, instructions, and activities. Use breaks to tease your audience about what is to come during the next break and everything in-between.

You want your audience excited to tune in. You provide an escape from their day, their work, or their ride home. Every day, every show, including every break, you need to be at your best. Air-time is money and you cannot waste it. Something needs to be happening all of the time. You are either playing music, commercials, promos, or you are entertaining. Teachers, this goes for us as well. Something with purpose is occurring at all times, or we are losing listeners—I mean, student engagement.

The Game of the Day

"Now it's time for the Game Of The Day. Today you have the chance to walk away with at least five bonus points, and all you need to do is be the first participant in today's Game of the Day. We need one volunteer to start the party. Thank you, Stacy, you just won two bonus points for volunteering."

Play some funky music right here so the students know what's coming. Break up the monotony, shake 'em up a little bit. An opportunity to win some bonus point is provided for all. If the entire class is good, everybody will win!

If you are really good, design the Game of the Day to relate to the show's content or events. For example, it is Taylor Swift's birthday, put together a Taylor Swift Fact-or-Fiction trivia challenge, or a Taylor Swift impersonation contest. Keep it simple, with a phrase that pays, like "When you hear the next Taylor Swift song, be caller number nine." A good game in radio can be an excellent way to include the listening audience in the show and allow them to experience being part of the show. Mix it up as well. Designate specific hours or days of the week for a variety of interactive games and prizes. It can be short, quick, simple—but anything to add some fun to the class, to break the day up, or to get the juices flowing to the brain once again!

To teach like a DJ, integrating the Game of the Day is a great bit. It can even be used at random. At that perfect moment when you just might be losing your students, fire the horn and start the Game of the Day. Maybe you know of an awkward transition as students progress from one part of the lesson to another and you want to get them excited. My favorite time for the Game of the Day is at the end of class if all work is done, and the students have been on-point all day. We will definitely be playing the Game of the Day for a chance to win bonus points. Students win the points and the teacher keeps the class engaged for the entire period. *Great game execution, class! Everybody just got bonused!*

You can go as big as you like with bonus points. Inflation may occur. Remember, you are the banker as well, so you'll be fine. Bonus points can be used for anything in my class. Put them on a test, a quiz, a project, a summative grade, a formative assignment - I do not care. Bonus points are earned when great projects are created or presented. Points for volunteers and when student engineers facilitate instruction. Students helping students is a bonus opportunity. Taking risks, accomplishing something for the first time and sharing with the class. Anything that ultimately improves the classroom environment or learning experience can and will be bonused!

Our bonus points roll over like AT&T. Save them for a rainy day. Save them for the last six weeks. It makes no difference to me because it is just another way to encourage learning at a higher level. It helps promote learning and our environment. Once you have earned your points I cannot take them away.

Early on, students who maintained a 100% at the end of the year, the bonus points were counted for the highest point total so students could hold the bonus point record. Bethany Kay Patton holds the semester-long bonus point total record to this day with 158 points. Basically, besides getting a 100% in the course, all she really won was this mention in the book.

Now, we have a Bonus Point Store that looks something like a video arcade shop to redeem your skeeball tickets. Candy, pens, pencils, fun jewelry, toys, games, posters, stickers, and a few big prize items for inspiration. Inflatable furniture, lava lamps, fidget spinners, and pizza parties, are some big prizes that students saved more than a hundred points to win. Keep in mind, you had to have extra points after your grade was 100% to spend points in the lounge. Jaxson Thornton, our year-long record holder at 182 points was able to cash in for the big prize his freshman year and went home for the summer with an inflatable couch. The best part is watching students who may not even care about their grades, but for a chance to win a few fun-size Snickers bars will work above and beyond.

News, Weather, & Traffic

There was absolutely no need for a traffic report in Stephenville, Texas, especially since our demographic stretched into Dublin, Hico, Ranger, Eastland, Morgan Mill, Lingleville, & Hamilton, Texas—all of which had even fewer traffic issues. But, on this one glorious day to work, as I was navigating a four-way stop with decent traffic, I came across a massive black shoe at the center of the intersection. Our very first traffic report from the KCUB Chopper would take place that day at 5:00 p.m., and every day thereafter.

This traffic report had nothing to do with real traffic except for typical underlying traffic themes, mixed with pop culture, current events, and community news. We used it to take typical, boring radio parts, like live reads or announcements, and present the content in a more engaging way. We invited celebrity guests like Randy Rogers to read the news in their own way. On national "Speak Like A Pirate Day," we read the news with a pirate accent. On Elvis's birthday, he interrupted the broadcast as he appeared from the heavens to give the traffic report from the KCUB Chopper.

To teach like a DJ, take any mundane, boring, methodical activity and find a way to whistle while you work. Don't make it cheesy and don't force it. Work to make it natural, fun, topical, relevant, and relatable. If you want the students to get the information, make it engaging. On "Speak Like a Pirate Day" I expect each and every teacher to introduce the lesson with their best pirate voice.

Interviews

One of my favorite interviews ever was with Seth McFarlane, the creator of Family Guy. He was promoting his new animated show *American Dad*, and I would have about ten minutes with him while

I was in LA at a Fox media junket. At the time, I had not watched any of the *Family Guy* episodes. But I did know that Seth was the show's creator, a writer, producer, director, and voiced many of the characters.

Before the interview, a handful of DJs from the top ten radio markets in the country got to watch a live reading by the cast of an entire episode of the new show. It was truly fascinating and entertaining. Even more impressive was watching Seth go back to back and sometimes between three different characters in a row, flawlessly and seemingly effortless. Seth and the cast were exceptional.

During any interview, I want to keep it real, and find a genuine appreciation or unique talking point that will differentiate my interview from the rest of the world's DJs. I want the interviewee to be engaged by the questions I ask. I would ask Seth the "Same 5 Questions," a bit we did with every celebrity interview on the morning show and one I later adopted in the classroom to "get to know" my students.

Same 5 Questions radio version for Mix 102.9 demographics:
1. If you could have dinner with any two celebrities, dead or alive, who would they be?
2. What is the best meal you can cook?
3. Favorite fashion accessory?
4. Favorite hair or grooming product?
5. What is the best sound effect you can make

The most important trait of Seth McFarlane from my perspective was his pure joy at doing something he loved. When you love what you are doing, the audience knows it and success will follow. We both loved what we were doing, and I enjoyed the fact that he was so down to earth, humble, and appreciative. The interview was great, the "Same 5 Questions" was hilarious, and my approach worked to ensure that the interview would provide some on-air content that was relevant to our demographic at Mix 102.9.

One of my favorite strategies to get to know my students is to ask them questions similar to the "Same 5 Questions." Really, it is more of a way for students to find a fun and comfortable way to begin sharing in class, getting to know each other, and creating a classroom environment conducive to sharing. I also adjust the questions for the particular class and demographic, just as I adjust the sharing and presentation strategies for different courses.

Same 5 Questions classroom edition:
1. If you could have dinner with any two celebrities, dead or alive, who would they be?
2. If you were a superhero, what would your power be?
3. Would you rather be president of the United States or lead singer in the best band? Why?
4. You are stranded on a deserted island. What is one item that you would take? Why?
5. Who is your favorite character on Stranger Things?

The activity for Speech-related classes is more like a live interview in front of the class, with opportunities for impromptu answers as the field of questions change for each student. Students in my Technology courses receive a digital copy of the questions, answer the questions, and turn them in using a variety of innovative paperless and collaborative ways to practice and apply how we make our classroom paperless. They can then share the answers for bonus points.

My first year at Frisco High School (also my first year as the Debate Coach), I reached out to other coaches and former students to provide demonstrations and/or question-and-answer sessions over Skype to train my students. The greatest benefit of our Skype interviews was the fact that we did not need to spend hundreds of dollars for travel, food, and team fees to get real practice. We even hosted the Debate team "scrimmages" against other schools online.

An interview may also relate to the specific instructional tool, the course, or the instructional goal. You can find a reason to reward the kids with a fun Skype session or presentation. Work to find a professional, celebrity, author, or former student to enhance your instruction with interviews. There are experts out there who know more than we do, and when we bring them in, we provide enhanced, engaging instruction for our students.

Interviews are great learning tools as well. Let the kids do the legwork and host your own "Skype & Tell." Challenge students to find and interview an expert in a field related to the instruction. Have them record outside of class, or Skype the interview live in the classroom. The research and preparation necessary to find a guest speaker, develop quality questions, and analyze the credentials of experts are great skills for students to practice and apply.

Sidekick

Big A, Cousin Brad, Red, Movies with Shane, Michael Beach, and the Linkster were all excellent sidekicks. Sidekicks always make the show easier, more fun and engaging. Having a sidekick enhances the energy in the room. If you are near me when the microphone is on, you just may end up being a sidekick.

Mr. Achberger—also known as Mr. A was the best classroom sidekick I have ever had to this day. Even more people will know Mr. A, from his own background in entertainment, prior to teaching, as the World Wrestling Entertainment (WWE) "Sign Guy." I did not know this until about halfway through the first semester, but once I did we were off to the races. He was known for making ridiculous signs calling out the biggest professional wrestlers and would often end up right in their face. This guy was more entertaining than me, and once he and I both understood each other, we co-created one of the most fun semesters of my teaching career.

Mr. A, with his WWE Sign Guy experience, was not scared of an audience, and he was welcome to participate in any of our discussions and activities. The entire class ended up loving Mr. A as much as any other teacher. He was hired to provide assistance to one student in our class, but was welcome to help all students in my class. He made our entire class better and that class has proved to be one of my favorites of all time.

We even retired his desk at the end of the year by bedazzling it to forever commemorate his extraordinary teaching in an end-of-year classroom desk retirement ceremony. He was assigned to work with a student in the classroom, but he went above and beyond and became part of our class and part of our learning experiences. Everyone loved Mr. A and our entire class was better because of his involvement.

If you stop by my classroom, there is a good chance you will become part of the activities. Do not think that you are just going to pop your head in and observe a student or teacher without getting your hands dirty. The classroom is not a show to watch. The classroom is an interactive learning experience and any guests are potential assets.

My student aides do real work as well. They can be wonderful sidekicks and valuable assets for keeping the classroom moving forward, as they have already graduated the course and know how the show flows. They know how the games are played. They know how the bonus points work. They can help sell an activity, project, or tool even better than the teacher. When you get the ball rolling, and the student aide cheers in happiness saying how much they loved that project, the class is already sold and ready to work. A good sidekick will make a class better.

Sports

I could give you some examples here about how sports stories are produced. About working as the Sports Director and having to go in on Sundays to interview multiple coaches in the Abilene area. I even have some terrible examples of me broadcasting baseball games and football games, where sometimes my best answer was "I don't remember," or "I don't know." I could even go into my athletic background, as it is a wonderful story and our high school team still holds the all-time total football yardage record for the history of our country. Bringing sports into the classroom mimics athletic training and competition for the mind.

Just like exercise and muscle groups, I want to keep the kids guessing, on their toes, and not knowing exactly what they will be getting into. From the moment they enter the classroom to the final bell, I want a learning frenzy occurring. I want students moving around, utilizing equipment, sharing, and collaborating. The teacher is like a coach in the middle of a game: constantly moving, assessing, drawing up plays, making game-time decisions. This is how the learning frenzy is monitored and controlled, and in turn enabling constant assessment of the students' learning.

Many radio studios are "stand up" with the idea that if the DJ is standing, the DJ will be more awake, upbeat, and exciting. I also remember my high school coaches never sitting down. If we were working so were they. I removed my desk from my classroom.

There is a stand-up desk for presentations and a table in the middle of the room if necessary for drawing up battle plans. I do not sit. I move around the room, checking progress, checking for understanding, and most importantly, motivating the students. I want high-fives. I want end zone celebration dances. I want "good jobs," "attaboys," "keep working hard," and one-on-one interaction with every student every day.

If you are thinking, *Well I won't have time for grading*, or *I won't have time for emails*—first, quit checking your emails during class. Other teachers will be mad at first, but once they know that you only check before school, during conference period, or after school, they will leave you alone. Now, you and your students have more freedom to learn and explore together. Grading occurs live in the classroom as the show is happening. Continuous assessments and improvements adjust the student's grade in real time and can coach the student toward a perfect score.

The desk is a symbol of laziness. Get away from it. Keep the energy moving, and positive. Play some music. Throw in some games. Have fun and make your class feel alive. I got rid of paper-based tests for two reasons. One, because they are not the best way to assess learning; and two, because I get extremely bored and hate a quiet classroom. If class gets boring or stale, maybe it is time to get the juices flowing again to inspire even more creative ideas. Put some basketball goals up. I have three. Buy a clip-on ping pong set-up and easily convert any desk into a glorious classroom ping pong table. Before broadcasting or writing, we often will play a quick game of ping pong as we think of topics and brainstorm. When you incorporate sports, the students do not even know they are working.

One time, I got so excited I flipped a table in the classroom. I'm telling you, this student's project, idea, or whatever was so great I had to commemorate the moment. The rest of the year, that classes' goal was to do something so great I would flip another table. High five, do an end zone dance, or body surf across a desk. Move, motivate, inspire, celebrate, and score big as you incorporate sports into your class. Your grading will be much easier. You will have more time to think of big ideas to incorporate in instructions. You will have more fun. Your students will have more fun, learn more, and create better projects. *"This has been your sports update. For KTCH 101.1, I'm B. J. Mercer. Back to you."*

Show Close

A good DJ will be just as passionate, and just as effective when closing the show. Ideally, the passion and energy during the show intro have continued with every push of the mic button. My show close was not always on point. When I accidentally kicked a Tarleton State University Conference Championship game off the air, with a minute left in the game, it was not the worst. Even the time I locked myself outside of our studio in Abilene, Texas at Kicker 107 during a McMurry University football broadcast, the only other key about ten minutes away at the program director's house, isn't really worthy.

My worst show close ever was at the end of an interview on an exceptionally busy day. Jason Boland, Randy Rogers, and Cross Canadian Ragweed were and are still some of the biggest names in Texas Music, and especially for our demographic at Texas 98 at that time. A four-hour show with three interviews from these guys sounds like a great show and much better than the reality of three interviews in the last hour, but that is when they showed up. Bands are known to go by their own schedule.

The Jason Boland interview was fine, as he was there by 6:00 pm. KCUB was not automated at this point, meaning that I would still play CDs, answer calls, run commercials, and facilitate the guests and their instruments, as they would play live. The main issue wasn't even anyone's fault. On Mondays, Wednesdays, and Fridays, I had a master's course at 7:00 pm, just down the road from our station. I could often close the show early around 6:50 and make it to class on time. This particular day the concern about being on time was exacerbated, since I would be taking a major test and I would have liked a few minutes to do some crash studying. Plus, I had some great questions written down somewhere in the studio and I needed a few seconds to locate them.

Randy Rogers was here and ready. Now, It was already 6:25pm, thirty-five minutes until testing time.

During the first break with Randy, I was not terrible and he began to play some live music. At this time, Cross Canadian Ragweed would appear through the large glass window, inside the radio station lobby, overlooking the studio. Like scientists in a lab, you could watch the DJs and artists as they performed live through the observation window.

This would be my 5th interview with CCR, and I guess they felt comfortable enough or thought it would be clever, as all four members mooned us from the other side of the glass. Just like the Care Bears cartoon from the eighties would line up and execute a Care Bear Stare. Randy and I were mooned by the power of four. I was proud of Randy though, he didn't miss a beat as he continued his live performance. For me, this was a sign of things to come. The interviews and show close would continue to get worse and the clock was ticking.

The remaining questions for Randy were boring, generic, and not my style. *If I could just find this list of interviews questions where I had written down during my show prep we would be set*, but there has not been a break in the chaos. By the time, I get rid of Randy, haul in Cross Canadian Ragweed, it would be 6:40. This was also one of those times when you really need to just relax and clear your mind, but this CD only has one minute and fifteen seconds left to play, the phones are ringing, one of the band members urinated on the plant in the lobby. I need to be on the road in ten minutes. And, where are my stupid questions?

My fifth and final interview ever with CCR would commence. At that time, this band was hands-down the favorite band of our demographic. I still couldn't find my questions, but I had hoped that I could jump start the interview by asking Cody Canada, the lead singer, a question I did remember about his brand new baby who was not yet even a month old. This would buy me some time to at least put together another solid question or two, or find the missing questions. It was all downhill from here. No more bands were coming in, we could knock this out like the professionals we had become over the years together. We were just one more break away.

Cody, my favorite, and also my very first interview on the radio about five years prior, had always taken care of me. Throughout the years he would invite me backstage. Often, a courtesy "shout out" during their performances. Certainly, he would have my back and answer this one question and give me at least a solid twenty seconds or so to prepare my next question and maybe, finally find my original questions.

When asked what it's like being a new father he said, "It's great, but I'm not the only one. Grady just had a baby, too." "Oh cool," I replied. Now let's see if Grady Cross, the lead guitarist can help me out. I just need some time to regroup here. And, Grady had been a part of this five-year relationship as well. Didn't they remember the famous Cross Canadian Turkey Shoot we did on the air together just a few years ago? "Well, Grady, I don't have any children, what it been like for you?" "Great," he said.

That was it. My brain was done, it just quit. It was as if I had been doing brain push-ups all day long and my brain muscle said that's it, you are on your own. It is 6:45, and I'm fifteen minutes away from a big test, we still have the show close to do together and I have an entire band staring at me. No one is saying anything.

I really do not remember anything at all from this point of the interview. Maybe someone else will interview Cody Canada about his worst interview ever and he will be able to fill in whatever I missed. He did not want to be at the radio station any more than I did at this point. I had a big test on the way and he had cold beer on the tour bus, chanting for him to return like an encore at his concert.

The show close would occur right now, it was my only way out of this situation and my last chance to make it out with any chance of taking the test on time. We would mention event times, location details, ticket info, websites, and social media. Thanks for stopping by, the next DJ will help you guys out, I gotta go.

Looking back, and almost immediately, I realized how I should have handled that interview. It could have been one of my best. And, it proved to be a significant lesson that I have tried to incorporate ever since on the air. It was simple too, I just needed to be real with my guests, and use the real-life situation as the content for the interview and include what was going on live, on and off the air—especially the test and even my missing questions.

I should have embraced the drama from the start. A real interview opportunity (learning experience) for all. Maybe Randy and I could go over some of my review questions for my business test. Listeners could call in with test-taking advice. Jason Boland could talk about his worst high school experience. Cross Canadian Ragweed could run the show themselves. I could even hand them the pop culture news of the day, or ask them to ask themselves questions they have never been asked before. We could call it *Ask Yourself*. Even let them read the sponsors, and do the office show close for the day, as I sat there and "studied" as part of the on-air bit. That would have been engaging! Even better, following the on-air crash course, study session, we would have had some excellent content to start the show the next day. We could promote a live call-in from Cody Canada to discuss the test results.

It was a good lesson for me. I may have tarnished my relationship with Cross Canadian Ragweed, but there is a good chance that Cody Canada will not even remember the interview - for many reasons not related to the interview.

From that point on, I would embrace the real-life situations and incorporate the issues into our content. And, I would never let the show close be as bad as that one. The show close is every bit as important to engage, inform, and entertain your audience as the show intro. You want your audience to have as many reasons as possible to return and to look forward to the next show. Get them excited to come back and stay tuned!

To teach like a DJ, recap the highlights at the end of every class. Talk about what incredible experiences have occurred in class that day, what is going on next class, and later in the week. Don't forget to mention the website for all course information, videos, podcasts, and ways to collaborate and share your incredible creations. Finally, throw in a quote of the day, joke, or a last-minute bonus opportunity to reward those going above and beyond outside of class exploring the related course content. It's just the best way to continue the momentum and ensure engaging instruction occurs from start to finish, between the bells and beyond.

I think most teachers take the time to reflect on the lesson. Give credit to those who stepped up that day. Most importantly, if you really want the students engaged, during the last few statements as the bell is ringing, you could end with the same strategies you used during your intro. You can say it, you can write it, but if you sing it they just might remember their homework. You will probably even get a shout out at the dinner table when they get home. Let's call it "Rap the Recap." Use Autorap and your content is automatically produced as if you are Kanye. End with the quote of the day, or word of the day. Something, to keep them tuned in, listening, engaged, and informed. 99.9% of the time this works. "87% of statistics are made up on the spot." For example, I just made up that statistic.

Today we close this show with the secret to teaching ...
When I first decided to leave radio and start teaching I visited one of my most incredible coaches from my junior high and high school experience. He helped me to get the ball rolling by providing some contacts and a healthy dose of motivation. I asked Coach Cervetto, then Principal at Henderson Junior High and now the Athletic Director of a new revitalized Dublin High School athletic program, "What is the best advice you can give me?" Coach Cervetto's answer was the most effective piece of

educational instruction I have ever received. Even to this day, after hundreds of staff development and professional development hours, half of a master's degree, four weeks of "New To The District" training, and my online emergency training and teacher certification course, no other piece of my formal educational training has been more valuable. I would even say it is the secret to teaching. It is almost too simple. And, trust me, Coach Cervetto is not known for brevity.

"Just let 'em know you care."

—Coach Bob Cervetto, Dublin ISD Athletic Director

ACKNOWLEDGMENTS

The only other experience that I can compare to ten years in radio, or nine in teaching, is eight years as a football player—six of those years in the program that accounted for Stephenville winning four Class 4A State Championships. The leadership, motivation, experience, and program was the fuel for my success in radio, in the classroom, as a Debate coach, and in life.

"Work hard dream big" was the message on a magnetic sign placed on my football locker in high school. Today, the original sign hangs on the dry erase board at the front of my classroom. The class website for students to access all of our missions is at www.workharddreambig.com.

I have incorporated into my daily life many lessons that I learned from Art Briles and his program. When his lessons and attitudes are practiced daily and integrated into your work ethic, you will be successful. Coach Briles influenced me and made me better every day of my eight years in football and has colored every day of my life since.

When I instruct, I am also a coach, with the goal of motivating my students to be working at their absolute best throughout the day, and beyond ... I teach like we're running the Art Briles' offense. It is fast and designed around the talent. I present our instruction fast, it's ever-changing and built for each student to be as successful as possible. The Art Briles' offense is designed to score often and in a hurry. If you teach like the Art Briles' offense is run, your kids are always moving, motivated, and learning.

Coaches

Thank you, Coach Cervetto. This man does care. He will let you know it and will keep you on track. He is always motivating and makes everyone around him better. He is a once-in-a-lifetime coach.

All of my high school coaches were difference makers. My success athletically and beyond, and incredible, once in a lifetime experiences, were only possible because of my coaches and the vision of Coach Art Briles. Thank you, Mike Copeland, Philip Montgomery, Randy Clements, Sean Lonergan, Randall Edwards, Eric Slaughter, Joseph Gillespie, Jeff Merket, Tommy Dunn, Johnny Bethea, Kelly Gilbert, Bob Couture, and Tom Black.

Teachers

I had some great teachers who helped me to find my ultimate career path. Donna Wesson inspired me as early as 6th grade and introduced some projects that made learning English fun. One project was the inspiration for The Bus Song—a song that has now been played on the radio and in many of my classes as a reward for my students. It was projects that you provided so often that showed me that teaching could be real: engaging and fun.

Sherry Crain, your classroom environment, and instructional design in your seventh-grade Speech class were what made me want to be a teacher.

Mrs. Diana Hassler, my eighth-grade speech teacher confirmed that I was on the right path and convinced me that I could one day make her famous.

Administrators

Dexter Dumas, I cannot thank you enough for your leadership, instruction, and motivation. You could have made or broke me as a first-year teacher and my first Assistant Principal. You gave me a foundation of confidence that inspired me to keep getting better. You set me up for success.

Sylvia Palacios, as Principal at Frisco High School, you allowed me to teach the way I thought was best. You ensured that we had what was necessary to be the best. Your school was always so efficient and effectively well run. It was easy to tell how much you cared for the students and staff. You believed in me when I was still learning, and that was inspirational.

Bruce Gearing, as Superintendent, you are leading a district of innovation in Dripping Springs. You encourage teachers to push the limits, explore, and create individualized learning experiences for our students. Dripping Springs High School and Dripping Springs ISD standout from the others and you are one of the reasons why we are all so successful. Thank you for allowing me to teach and for our students to explore. I am a huge fan.

Joe Burns, thank you for the support, believing in me, and allowing our students to learn in new and innovative ways. As principal, you make Dripping Springs High School an excellent environment for teachers and students. The principal can make or break a school and you make our school one of the best and a reason I will happily make the drive from south Austin.

Students

Thank you to all of my former students. We took many chances, and you guys always stepped up and made me look good. I may have had some good ideas along the way, but these kids made sure that we were successful. A special thank you to some exceptionally fearless students Symone Gamble, Ajani Brown, Yana Gololabova, Sandra Sillia, Matt Areté, Christine Ingram, Amber Rosamond, Jessica Bathea, Monica Adelle, Mahek Sajan, and Jaxson Thornton.

Radio

Norma Savage, thank you for giving me my first job in radio. You were the General Manager at KCUB radio. I was a college kid who made mistakes, but you were patient and kind. I learned so much about the business just by being in close quarters with you.

Dina De La Rocha, Victoria Snee, Tony Zazza, Crystal Fox, Jody Lee Caudle, and Pete Garcia were generous and influential in my radio background and career. Thank you for your help on my journey.

Book Editing and Cover Design

Jess Habermann and Cider Spoon Stories, thank you for your help editing this book. You are excellent, and if anyone needs an editor I recommend you.

Izzy Avena, you did an amazing job working your magic on the cover. You are a gifted artist and a wonderful student who makes a classroom better.

Dominic Gearing, you are talented at so many things including photography. You made me look good on the back cover. I look forward to seeing what else you create in your high school career.

Friends

To all of my friends that have believed in me and supported me in many ways over the years. I do not get to see any of you as much as I would like to but I am appreciative of our friendship. Thank you Cam Fergason, JW Boren, Kevin Burton, Jack Hodges, Kelan Luker, Jimmy Ferrazas, Matt Tinklenberg, Felix Alvarado, Brady Chandler, Josh Martin, Matt Magin, Summer Langford, Justin Monk, Jancy Briles, the Borens, Nick Eatman, Jen Riddlebarger, John Adams, and Nadia Bening.

Family

Luane Anders, Karen Turvey Grubbs, The Mercer, Turvey, and Collins family, my supportive aunts and uncles, amazing cousins, and those I have missed lots of time with pursuing my career in radio, traveling, and writing this book - I love you all tremendously and thank you for always supporting me, and making me feel loved and welcomed.

Adam Mercer, my younger brother who is so much fun to be around. You have always been there on and off the air. You always make me laugh and get all my jokes too. You make life better and I love every minute we get to be around each other.

Jamie Mercer, my little sister, taught her big brother how to travel. She taught me how to be adventurous. To explore other cultures, learn languages, and find some of the best things in life. You have made your older brother a better person.

Most importantly, the greatest thanks of all to Jim and Wanda Mercer. I have the best parents. I could not ask for more caring, understanding, compassionate, supportive, intelligent, trusting, reliable, and loving parents. Without their foundation, I would not have been able to take in all of the experiences that shaped my background and young life. Their philosophies are the deepest foundation of this book, and many educational strategies are a reflection of how I was raised. Without such an incredible foundation, I would not have had the base to build upon, that led to my career on and off the air, and writing this book would not have been possible. I was raised to do this, but never told to. A book could be written about my parents' strategies for raising children. My parents' careers were and are in education from coaching to counseling, teaching, and administration from elementary grade level to the university system level. My parents are educators, and the education they gave me is priceless, and I could not have asked for better parents. I love you, mom and dad.

ABOUT THE AUTHOR

For ten years, across north Texas from Stephenville to Abilene and Dallas, B. J. Mercer worked in almost every part of the radio business. As a DJ, Program Director, Producer, and Sports Director, Mercer worked his way from the bottom to the top in radio. At Mix 102.9 Dallas, as a morning show DJ and producer, Mercer produced one of the most highly rated morning shows in the top five radio market in the country. Radio personalities specialize in keeping their audience engaged!

In 2008, Mercer began his new career as a classroom teacher. In that first year, Mercer earned Teacher of the Month and was then awarded Teacher of the Year runner-up. During years two and three, Mercer instructed professional development, his students' projects were selected to the top five projects in Frisco ISD (FISD) and his instructional strategies were showcased at Texas Classroom Educators Association (TCEA) conferences. Mercer's classroom was selected from FISD as a model for the integration of instructional technology. School districts outside of FISD were invited and observed Mercer's instructional design, instructional strategies, and new technology integration.

Mercer has taught in four different school districts, worked at six different schools and has taught more than fourteen different courses for grades 6 through 12. With only nine years in the classroom, Mercer has been nominated for Teacher of the Year four times and, most recently, at Dripping Springs Independent School District (DSISD), Mercer has also been recognized as Teacher of the Term by the DSISD Education Foundation. At this same time, he was presented the *Above & Beyond Award* from the DSISD School Board as he instructed eight new courses and his students built the school's first radio station.

Like your favorite radio personalities who keep you listening, wanting more, excited to be part of the process, and ready for your chance to win, Mercer keeps his students engaged with creative instructional design, motivating activities, innovative instructional technology, and opportunities for self-discovery. This approach guarantees that each student is *tuned in*!

At first, Mercer believed radio was his dream vocation. Nine years ago, he realized the profession that he loves most is teaching and he has been teaching like a DJ ever since. The school districts, courses, and demographics have all changed but students are the common denominator. Teaching like a DJ has worked every step of the way!

Made in the USA
Columbia, SC
08 June 2018